Teaching Research Processes

CHANDOS
INFORMATION PROFESSIONAL SERIES

Series Editor: Ruth Rikowski
(email: Rikowskigr@aol.com)

Chandos' new series of books is aimed at the busy information professional. They have been specially commissioned to provide the reader with an authoritative view of current thinking. They are designed to provide easy-to-read and (most importantly) practical coverage of topics that are of interest to librarians and other information professionals. If you would like a full listing of current and forthcoming titles, please visit our website www.chandospublishing.com or email wp@woodheadpublishing.com or telephone +44(0) 1223 499140.

New authors: we are always pleased to receive ideas for new titles; if you would like to write a book for Chandos, please contact Dr Glyn Jones on email gjones@chandospublishing.com or telephone number +44(0) 1993 848726.

Bulk orders: some organisations buy a number of copies of our books. If you are interested in doing this, we would be pleased to discuss a discount. Please contact on email wp@woodheadpublishing.com or telephone +44(0) 1223 499140.

Teaching Research Processes

The faculty role in the development of skilled student researchers

WILLIAM B. BADKE

CP

CHANDOS
PUBLISHING

Oxford Cambridge New Delhi

Chandos Publishing
Hexagon House
Avenue 4
Station Lane
Witney
Oxford OX28 4BN
UK
Tel: +44 (0) 1993 848726
Email: info@chandospublishing.com
www.chandospublishing.com

Chandos Publishing is an imprint of Woodhead Publishing Limited

Woodhead Publishing Limited
80 High Street
Sawston
Cambridge CB22 3HJ
UK
Tel: +44 (0) 1223 499140
Tel: +44 (0) 1223 832819
www.woodheadpublishing.com

First published in 2012

ISBN 978-1-84334-674-6 (print)

ISBN 978-1-78063-305-3 (online)

© W.B. Badke, 2012

British Library Cataloguing-in-Publication Data.
A catalogue record for this book is available from the British Library.

Typeset by RefineCatch Limited, Bungay, Suffolk
Printed in the UK and USA.

Contents

Preface: my journey into research processes		ix
Acknowledgements		xv
About the author		xvii
1	**Defining research processes**	**1**
	Average faculty expectations	2
	Common definitions	7
	The capabilities actually required by students	9
	Keeping the goal consistent with higher education's mission	21
	What are we looking for?	22
	The idea of research processes	24
2	**Research ability inadequacies in higher education**	**25**
	Where the problem starts	27
	University students and information skills – an overview	32
	Information literacy of senior undergraduate/ graduate students	36
	The information literacy of faculty members	44
	The bottom line: information illiteracy in academia	46
	Notes	48

3   **Research processes and faculty understanding**   **49**

The understanding gap   50

The university administration gap   55

The silo problem   56

The perpetuated experience (osmosis) gap   57

Faulty assumptions about students and
technology   60

Faculty culture   62

Faculty perception of librarians   67

The hesitation of accrediting bodies   67

Conclusion   68

Note   69

4   **Current initiatives in research processes**   **71**

Development of standards among academic
librarians   74

Remedial instruction   78

Credit-based courses   81

Instruction through the curriculum   84

The essential failure of all such initiatives   86

5   **The role of disciplinary thinking in research
processes**   **91**

The development of scholarly ability within a
discipline – content and process   93

Learning about versus doing   107

The difference between disciplinary experts
and undergraduates   109

The radical shift in thinking demanded for
effective research processes instruction to
university students   113

6	Research processes in the classroom	115
	Essential goals	116
	Congruence with active learning and constructivism	116
	Required thinking and process skills	123
	Required changes in teaching patterns	126
	The new classroom	131
	What about content?	136
7	Tentative case studies in disciplinary research process instruction	139
	The humanities	141
	The social sciences	147
	The sciences	153
	Professional programs	158
	Conclusion	161
8	Research processes transforming education	163
	The educational task of the professor	164
	Departmental planning for teaching research processes	170
	University planning for teaching research processes	175
9	Resourcing the enterprise	179
	The question of priorities	180
	Realigning academic librarians	183
	Taking a grassroots approach	185
	Buy-in at the top	187
	What resources do we need?	190
10	Conclusion	191
	References	195
	Index	221

Preface: my journey into research processes

It began with a revelation. After a two-year term in Africa teaching in a theological school, I took a Master of Library Science degree and started a dual appointment as Associate Professor and Librarian at a theological school. This unusual combination of roles – librarian and associate professor – led me to pay more attention to student research papers (undergraduate and graduate) than I had done in the past. Were my students optimizing library resources? Could inadequacies in the library collection be identified in student essays?

I wasn't expecting a revelation, but I was struck by one anyway. One day, I realized that *my students did not know how to do research*. If you're an academic, you may now be rolling your eyes in recognition that my epiphany was so obvious, even so mundane. Academics are well used to shabby, shallow research papers dashed off in the dark hours after midnight and proofread over breakfast cereal, if at all. We sigh in dismay at banal literature reviews that miss most of the literature and lack even a rudimentary goal. We have come to believe that many of our students are unmotivated, refusing to use whatever critical thinking their deity blessed them with. They do research badly, and we respond with low grades, sort of a passive-aggressive revenge game played out on every campus in the world.

But none of this speaks to my revelation – My students did not *know* how to do research. Motivation and procrastination aside, *they simply did not know what they were doing*. They were like clumsy bears at a dinner party, trying to play nice but knowing that a mess would ensue. My students were lost when it came to handling information, from beginning to end. The only conceivable reason why any research papers came out of them at all was either that they spent so many hours blundering through their process that something had to emerge, or they seized the first resources they could find and dashed off their assignments quickly, so as not to prolong the pain of working at a hostile, alien task. Sadly, it is often difficult for a professor to discern the difference, because a mediocre paper is easy to fudge.

The next revelation I encountered, soon after the first one, was that most of my fellow professors, me included, were doing little or nothing to help our students. To be sure, we were still assigning research projects, giving stern warnings about plagiarism and proper format, and telling our students that we wanted deep, critical thinking. But we were consistently sending them out into the research project wilderness like naïve Hansels and Gretels destined to be baked and eaten by the wicked witch.

Now, some 25 years later, I am still convinced of the truth of my revelation – most students do not know how to do research. While some things have changed, none of them are for the better.

The world's knowledge base has transformed itself from print to an increasingly digital format. The information environment in which we live has changed dramatically since the late 1980s, revolutionizing the way in which we function within it. Doing any sort of informational research today demands that we have a solid grasp of our new electronic environment, its search tools, the types of information we need to handle, and the methods of evaluation demanded to determine quality and relevance. The widely varied digital nature of the new information environment has made information-based research vastly more complicated than it was even in the 1980s.

Truth to tell, our students never did know how to do research well and we academics never did all that much to help them. But now that technology has made the information world many times more complex than it was, we have a whole generation of current and upcoming students who are just lost. What is even more chilling is the fact that academia itself has not yet recognized the problem.

The premise of this book is a simple one – the most glaring error in higher education's current struggle for relevance is our blindness to the fact that our students do not know how to do research, and we are not doing enough to help them. In this, I do not mean simply that our students turn in bad research papers. Rather, our students are not being taught how to handle information with understanding and skill. Either we sincerely believe we are already teaching them how to do this or we assume that our students will learn it on their own. But the plain and simple fact is that they are not doing so.

We are not teaching them how to formulate information problems, how to acquire the information they need to engage significantly with those problems, how to evaluate that information and how to use it effectively. This oversight is leaving our students unable to function as they should in the new information economy. The result is costly and damaging to most workplaces, not to mention the disservice we do to those who graduate from our institutions believing they are educated, when they are not.

Let's consider this from another standpoint. My premise is this: *Our students do not know how to do research*. If that is true – and I plan to demonstrate that it most certainly is –

then we are failing to meet our own purpose as educators. We want to graduate students who understand their field and handle the information within it effectively, efficiently and ethically; we want students who are strong critical thinkers and lifelong learners, able to navigate the knowledge tasks required of their lifework. Yet our students are graduating without ever learning how to handle the information that will be their stock in trade.

Let me make an even more provocative statement: *Students who do not know how to do research are not educated students.* They may have a keen grasp of factual data; they may have memorized enough of the terminology to pass their exams and speak with seeming sophistication about their fields. But they are not educated, any more than filling your car with gas means that it knows how to make its own journey home.

In a world in which Wikipedia can help any intelligent person sound superficially like a university graduate, factual knowledge is a cheap commodity and can no longer be used as a substitute for a real education. Educating students these days is not just about knowledge transfer from the professor's brain to the student's, but also about knowledge navigation – about making something fresh out of what you know, about problem-solving in which information is less a treasure than a tool.

This book will contend that a student who does not know how to do research – identify a problem, determine the information needed to solve that problem, acquire that information skillfully, sift through and evaluate what has been found, then use that information critically to address the problem – is indeed not an educated person.

The irony is that today's higher education does everything but engage with this foundational skill and understanding gap. We teach students how to parrot our knowledge base. We teach them how to mimic the particular writing conventions of our discipline. We show them experimental method in the sciences and social sciences (while rarely having them perform any significantly original experiments until they are in graduate school). We teach them how to obey the rules of bibliographical format. We tell them to think critically (without giving them more than token exercises in doing so). But we do not help them learn how to handle information and genuinely engage in research.

Librarians like myself know the truth, even if we have not been able to communicate the seriousness of the situation to the rest of academia. We librarians see the challenge every day – hopeless, struggling students who have little clue where to begin or what to look for as they do their "research projects." In fact, there is a large literature on this topic, which is usually labeled "information literacy," but it is located within library literature, not that of higher education.

Faculty members, in turn, dismayed at the poor quality of student "research," are loath to waste time writing extensive comments on student papers. Thus professors are assigning fewer and fewer research projects, opting for reaction pieces, journals, book reviews and quizzes. Students who still do any significant research writing turn in papers with bibliographies that have a strong emphasis on web pages. We give them low marks and tell them to straighten up, but they don't. Why not? Because we have not determined how to teach them good methods, and students do not learn how to do research unless they are taught. So, instead of improving their research abilities, we tend to opt for giving them fewer opportunities to do research.

Is the problem as serious as all that? This question could be interpreted in a number of ways:

- Do our students really not know how to do research or is information handling a skill they inevitably acquire over time?

- Does skillful research really matter for students who are for the most part going into careers that demand few or no academic research projects?

- Is the new information environment so complex that special skills are needed by our students, without which they would be uneducated?

The following chapters will address these questions before moving toward a plan to address the problem.

Acknowledgements

The author wishes first to acknowledge the supportive team of librarians and library staff at Norma Marion Alloway Library of Trinity Western University. Your creativity and encouragement are truly exceptional.

The faculty of Trinity Western University and its graduate theological program, Associated Canadian Theological Schools, have welcomed my involvement in their lives and have provided significant insight into learning how to teach research processes effectively. Thank you.

Finally, thanks to my family, Rosemary, Shawn, Jordan, and grandson Zackery, for encouraging my pursuit of teaching research processes.

About the author

William B. Badke is Associate Librarian for Associated Canadian Theological Schools and Information Literacy at Trinity Western University, Langley, BC, Canada. Since 1985, he has taught information literacy for credit to undergraduate and graduate students. His online graduate information literacy course was the first of its kind. Working closely with faculty members, he frequently offers guidance to enable them to take a greater role in teaching research processes to students. He is the author of numerous articles on information literacy and of the widely used textbook, *Research Strategies: Finding your Way through the Information Fog*, 4th edn. (Bloomington, IN: iUniverse. com, 2011).

1

Defining research processes

Abstract: While professors hope for critically argued and well-referenced research projects from their students, the results are generally disappointing, leading to a lowering of requirements. Disciplines do add nuances to the various research processes, but there is a common core involving use of a question or hypothesis, acquisition and use of information, and a 'quest.' In working with information (that which informs) and doing research, students need the following capabilities: An understanding of today's world of information, the ability to identify problems and acquire the information to solve them, significant technological knowledge, and critical thinking and evaluation abilities. These capabilities are congruent with the dominant mission of higher education. 'Research processes' represent the procedural side of the academic disciplines. Students require a rigorous complex of understandings and skills in order to find success in their research.

Key words: acquire information, critical thinking, disciplines, hypotheses, identify problems, quest, research questions, technological knowledge, today's world of information.

Student research, whether it is embodied in a classic research paper in the humanities or a literature review in the social sciences or sciences, has always been an awkward and troubling phenomenon. From the standpoint of the average student, a research project is a monumental task to be avoided until the deadline looms and only then to be addressed as if taking a bitter pill for an unknown illness. Professors, likewise, have grown to believe that it is virtually impossible to get good research by students, so that expectations have been lowered to meet the maximum that can be expected ("three books and two journal articles, no websites"). So difficult has it become to get good research by students, that many professors are now opting for other types of assignments. Why bother with student research papers when the product is so unlike published writing in the discipline that calling it "research" becomes a ridiculous misnomer?

There are excellent reasons, however, not to give up on student research. Done well, if that is possible, it engages students in a deeper level of inquiry than does rote learning of facts. It is also a doorway, as we will see, to inviting students into the discipline being taught rather than just familiarizing them with the discipline's content.

Average faculty expectations

What, then, are faculty members actually saying about student research? What do they expect, and what do they receive?

Many faculty members view "writing" as a significant issue for undergraduates and graduate students. Singleton-Jackson, Lumsden and Newsom (2009), for example, reviewed a fairly extensive literature devoted to measuring undergraduate and graduate student writing. Their study concluded that academic writing, especially at graduate level, is complex and hard to measure. They argued that, not only are there necessary analytical and critical thinking skills, but there is also a required understanding of the nature of such writing, including its mechanics.

These researchers administered the SAT II: Writing Test, Part B, to Master's and doctoral students studying in higher education programs. The SAT II, which measures discernment of academic writing conventions and use of language to derive meaning, scored these graduate students at *not significantly higher levels than pre-college students*. Such a study, while instructive in itself, is a strong example of the significant emphasis that academics place on the conventions and language of writing itself. The authors showed little concern for other research attainments such as strength of research questions or theses, ability to develop strong bibliographies, and actual use of research resources in projects developed by students.

What, then, are the common expectations for student research papers among faculty? Greasley and Cassidy (2010) polled a number of professors at Bradford University in the UK and found a common core: Faculty members expected critical analysis and argumentation with supporting evidence, signs that assignment guidelines had been followed, good representation of the conventions required in research papers (structure, grammar and style, referencing), and so on. Interestingly, structural, grammatical and referencing issues received 56 percent of the comments, ranking them ahead of critical thinking. This gives the impression that faculty are more frustrated with poor presentation than poor thinking. The researchers suggested, however, that faculty members may be considering presentation to be a marker for underlying thought processes. Sloppy papers speak of sloppy minds and shallow thinking.

Maclellan (2004) identified the following faculty expectations: an argued position, use of sources to address that position, analysis of principles and purposes, and some sort of professional/practical outcome. She found that less than 10 percent of a collection of 40 student essays that professors had assigned high grades showed the highest levels of critical thinking.

One way of analyzing the disparity between what faculty members hope for and what they receive is to study the fit between faculty expectations and college students' mastery of the roles they need to take in order to meet those expectations. Collier and Morgan (2008) found that faculty expected students to follow the directions in research assignments, use acceptable grammar and style, and cite their sources correctly. Yet, even in such basic matters, the consensus of faculty members studied was that students often failed to grasp what was required of them. One professor commented, "They just don't get it." Students, in turn, said that they had received no actual training in producing research papers and faculty instructions were not detailed enough to make clear what was expected.

Faculty members' expectations tend to decrease as a result of their past experiences of student production. Avdic and Eklund (2010) demonstrated that professors generally expected a poorer result than did their students. Professors were in the main highly negative on most measures of student performance. Their students believed that professors overemphasized the role of scientific papers (as opposed to easier-to-understand studies) and that academic research skills are really only for the benefit of meeting professorial expectations. Students tended to see their actual search abilities as good but thwarted by databases that were intentionally not user-friendly.

What we appear to have here is a disconnection between how professors view student research production and what students believe they are accomplishing. While professors find their expectations generally are not being met, students think they are more skilled than their production demonstrates, while attempting to play by the rules, though not really understanding them, and not performing up to acceptable levels.

Bury (2011) found consistent faculty disappointment with student research ability, particularly in evaluating resources, avoiding plagiarism and citing sources, though less emphasis was placed on student inability to identify information needs and find that information effectively. The latter skills, from an abundance of other research studies, are points of challenge for most students, though the faculty members in Bury's study did not recognize the problem.

A certain amount of damaging circularity results. Students believe they are doing good work while faculty become accustomed to work that is inadequate. This, in turn, leads to lowered faculty expectations, which, in the eyes of students, is discerned as a lowering of demands upon them. Thus, these students do less rigorous work, and professors accept increasingly minimal quality research projects under the assumption that the average student's work is not capable of meeting higher expectations. We commonly see a pattern in newer professors in which they demand much of their students at first, then experience student rebellion or "underwhelming" performance, and lower their demands in succeeding years.

Valentine (2001), in a series of studies, found that the paramount concern of many students doing research papers was discerning "what the professor wants." That is, students were writing for the grades they received and believed that meeting professorial expectations was the key to receiving those grades. While they were quite willing to acknowledge their own failings, they blamed the professor if their low grades were seen as resulting from poor instructions or unreasonable restrictions placed upon their projects.

Professors, in turn, often had rather vague goals related to student projects, viewing them as learning experiences or attempts to learn how to participate in the discourse of the discipline. Grading criteria, based on faculty perceptions of student ability and commitment, were often changeable and subjective to the professor's experience with each student. Overall, professors were looking for "legitimate effort" in student research projects. When objective requirements for such an effort were made plain to students, they were satisfied. When there were no such stated requirements or the requirements were vague, students were unhappy.

A salient "from the trenches" perspective comes from the following anonymous (verbatim) response to a blog posting by a graduate nursing student:

> As a full time college student i am constantly asked to do research papers; sometimes on things i know very little about and could really care less. When i go into wright a paper for a class it is approached a lot different than my personal writing. There is a constant worry of being punished for plagiarizing because most subjects have been researched by many different people and they're only so many ways that you can word the same thing. The traditional research paper guide line should be abandoned. Why can't i make a point without having someone i have to cite? What makes that person creditable, the person he cited? It's just a big domino effect of who's creditable. When given a paper i believe the student should have total free rein on what he is to say. Yes, sources are needed but the citing and following MLA guidelines are not. Another of the problems that was mentioned in the blog post was that students find a book or topic they are enthusiastic about but they have to change the topic because they cannot find enough sources to cite what they may already know or have in their heads what they want to say. i have personally had

to change topics for the exact reason. i have also wrote argumentative papers arguing the side i disagree with just because it was a lot easier to argue that side. That's crap that students are writing on what they don't believe just so they can make their papers long enough and have proper MLA citations. (Response to Barbara Fister [Anonymous], 2011)

This belligerent and somewhat plaintive rant reveals some very pertinent issues surrounding the emphasis on student writing. We see in this student someone trying to succeed at a task for which he/she has been given all the rules without the explanations. *Why do I have to cite people? What gives them such special status? I can't find enough sources anyway. Why all the style rules? Why does academic writing kill creativity?*

Faculty expectations may well include such elements as critical thinking, a keen understanding of how to write in the discipline and a modicum of adherence to style, along with a watchful eye for plagiarism, but the problem is much bigger than this. What we are seeing is a wholesale misunderstanding by many students of the essential goals of academic research. Students are writing to rules set out by their professors without having much of a grasp of why those rules are there or what are the higher goals of the research process.

Common definitions

Definitions of "research" itself and "student research" in particular are many and varied. We have seen some of them embodied in the faculty expectations just examined. In general, while being somewhat simplistic, "student research" is commonly viewed as sending students out to address a topic with a keen eye to resources provided by scholars in the field. While not as often actually found to be the case, faculty retain at least a faint hope that the topic will be expressed as a research problem which demands that evidence be gathered, analysis (critical thinking) be done, and some sort of proposed solution be presented.

There are, of course, disciplinary nuances that modify the common definitions of research in general and student research in particular. A good historian would not consider any project as research if it did not address primary sources and provide rigorous analysis involving interpretation of those sources or a challenge of existing views about its subject matter. A scientist generally would not consider anything as research that did not involve a hypothesis and some sort of experimental or observational procedure. How, in the midst of such diversity as is found in the disciplines, can we speak of research at all, if we are referring to a singular process we expect our students to perform?

The fact is that we cannot. Disciplinary thinking always informs and modifies the research process, thus creating *research processes*. Yet there is a common core. First, all research that moves beyond mere description demands some sort of research problem, whether expressed as a question or a hypothesis. Second, research involves the acquisition and judicious use of relevant information. Here, the historian with a focus on primary sources, and their secondary accompaniments, has at least something in common with a scientist who must perform a literature review prior to determining a procedure to test a hypothesis. Information provides a common core to every research process even when the nature of that information is diverse. Third, all research that is more than descriptive in nature, requires a "quest," a search for something that is beyond what is already known or understood.

The argument may thus be made that "student research" is something of an oxymoron since what students do is predominantly derivative and secondary, making use of the work of others but contributing little that is original or advances the discipline. That is what we might expect, however, because students are students. They are inexperienced in the process, lacking the knowledge and sophistication of their professors who actually do "genuine research." This distinction between genuine research and student research, however, is unfortunate, since the essence of what we call "student research" is inevitably an imitation of what professors do, an attempt to embark upon a similar road without yet having the knowledge, skills and sophistication of seasoned researchers. To dismiss "student research" as not meeting the criteria of real research is to doom students never to learn how to become researchers. Such a gap becomes, as we will see, detrimental to their education and future careers.

We thus recognize diversity in the various disciplinary forms of research, while arguing that there is a common core that embodies defining a research problem, using information to address that problem, and creating an overall sense of "quest" that intends to move the researcher beyond what currently exists, even if that quest is followed inexpertly. "Student research," as inadequate as it often seems to be, is still research, even if it mimics the professional version to a large degree.

The capabilities actually required by students

What, then, do students actually need to accomplish to meet the highest expectations of their professors? The common term used to summarize the required capabilities, at least in the world of library and information science, is "information literacy," which we have re-expressed as ability with "research processes." Not only is information literacy a more significant need than most academics acknowledge, but it involves complex understandings and skills. In what follows, we will predominantly use the term "information literacy," because it is the label applied to the concept in the literature. Later we will refer more to ability with "research processes," as we move the concept into the disciplines, where it finds its best expression.

Bundy (2002) saw information literacy as "the key competency for the 21st century." Andretta (2007) described it as "the functional literacy of the 21st century." Is this mere hyperbole, or does information literacy have the potential to achieve first place in the competencies of educated people? The answer to that question really depends upon what we mean by this potentially nebulous term, "information literacy." What, indeed, are we meaning when we describe someone as an information-literate person?

Initially, let's define "information" itself. While simplistic, we can argue that information is that which informs. Whether it is verbal or auditory or visual, information is grist for the mill, the foundation of what we think about and know. It is genuine if it truly informs and mere data if it adds nothing to whatever subject matter we are dealing with. These days, it is important to recognize that information can come in many forms, from print to audio to video, and to be carried on a variety of media, from a hard cover book to a PDF to an iPad to a YouTube video. Though both simplistic and rather nebulous, I believe it's best to leave what we mean by "information" rather broad and allow it to be defined by its function – to inform.

Moving to the concept of information literacy, Webber and Johnston (2006) engaged the concept of the "learning organization" introduced by Pedler, Burgoyne and Boydell (1991), to argue:

> If organisations are truly to "learn" then they need employees who are able to identify when they need to learn, who can find out what the opportunities are for learning, and are able to find, use and communicate information as an integral part of their learning. (Webber and Johnston, 2006, p. 47)

This is the essence of information literacy and of the information literate person – someone who can harness information in order to grow or learn.

But it involves a great deal more than a set of skills. In today's information environment, it begins with understanding the nature of our knowledge base. It then demands sufficient critical ability to be able to identify a problem and crystallize a statement or question that sets the path to a solution. Further, it calls for skills to acquire the needed information. It assumes then that, once having appropriated information, there will be an ability to evaluate it critically, and to understand its biases, shortcomings and erroneous assumptions. Finally, the information-literate person will be able to relate found resources to other information, sifting out the wheat from the chaff, and using the resulting best information and evidence ethically to provide an effective solution to the identified problem.

Understanding today's world of information

All good research starts with epistemology. Epistemology is not the study of what we know but of *how we know what we know*, i.e., what are our sources of knowledge, where do they come from, in what forms are they transmitted to us, and why would we find one source more credible/usable than another?

For most subject specialists, epistemology is second nature and rarely if ever needs to be contemplated. Those who work with the information of their disciplines on a daily basis do not need to ask where that information came from or why it takes the forms it does. Nor do they think much about why some sources are more credible than others. They know how research is done in their field, how it is transmitted, and what is considered important or unimportant. For the average student, however, the knowledge base of most disciplines is a mystery filled with strange literatures published on the basis of incomprehensible, often unwritten, rules. Let us consider first the challenges that the newer modes of information present to the kinds of skilled research that professors hope to get from their students.

The average student comes from an environment in which concept of a "voice of authority" is becoming increasingly muted, making the restrictions of peer review, accepted forms of discourse, and rigorous criteria for evidence, as foreign as would be the sudden implementation of a dictatorship in an open, peace-loving democracy. For most students, epistemology seems not to be an issue at all – information on any topic is out there for the taking (generally found on the World Wide Web with a Google search). These days, we can even publish our own "information" to add to the mix. To impose rules on what is acceptable information and what is not just seems to be an abuse of power (see the nursing student comment in our introduction, above).

Dede (2008) has argued that Web 2.0 (as typified, for example, by Wikipedia) has created a "seismic shift in epistemology" in which the classical role of the expert who serves as a guardian of knowledge is replaced by collective agreement. While, admittedly, experts could be biased and self-serving, Dede does not see changing one epistemology (the creation of information by experts) for the other (information by collective agreement) as beneficial. Nor does he find the alternative helpful for educators – simply resisting all forms of Web 2.0. He writes: "This refusal to acknowledge the weaknesses of the Classical perspective and the strengths of Web 2.0 epistemologies is as ill-advised as completely abandoning Classical epistemology for Web 2.0 meaning-making" (ibid., p. 81). So the two perspectives will probably continue to live in tension, and the information-literate person must understand the pros and cons of each.

Closely related to epistemology is the concept of "classification," that is, the ways by which we create an organized representation of knowledge, breaking it into hierarchies, fitting it into categories, and so on. Examples of classification include the academic division of knowledge into "disciplines" and "subdisciplines." Found here as well are various hierarchical ways of organizing knowledge such as Britannica's Propaedia or library classification systems, which begin with broader categories and create sub-categories in the shape of an inverted tree. The purpose of classification is simple – we humans cannot deal with vast amounts of undifferentiated data. Knowing how data is organized by those who most often use it is foundational to understanding information in any discipline.

Here the work of Elmborg (2006) is very helpful. He argues that truly "critical information literacy" involves an understanding of the workings of various classification systems and the ways in which they produce "knowable reality and universal truth" (ibid., p. 197). Learning such systems, however, does not mean acceptance of the worldview behind them. For Elmborg, this learning task involves recognizing that knowledge is the result of "socially negotiated epistemological processes and the raw material for the further making of new knowledge" (ibid., p. 198). Knowing that peer review tends to maintain the status quo, and that classifications of knowledge develop disciplinary modes of thinking, are crucial elements of what Elmborg describes as "critical information literacy" (ibid., p. 198).

Critical information literacy amounts, ultimately, to understanding how knowledge is constructed as a result of various cultural forces (Lloyd, 2010) and knowing how we make sense of that knowledge by the ways in which it is organized. The information literate student is not only knowledgeable about classification but learns to be a critic of it, recognizing that classification, like information itself, is created from specific cultural emphases and biases.

Students need to understand how the information they have is structured in order to learn how to organize information for themselves. Grappling with reams of data requires not just the skill of appreciating where it came from and what is its nature, but also knowing how to differentiate within the data the categories that can be used to organize it. This, for the information handler, may mean both weeding out irrelevancies and organizing what is left into schools of thought or other categories intended to make it manageable. Our society's fascination with the quantity and speed of information needs to be replaced by an emphasis on structuring information. The ability to organize, find meaning, and preserve information is a key to using it effectively.

But teaching epistemology is not nearly as challenging as it appears to be. It amounts, within the classroom, to illuminating the knowledge base of the particular discipline under discussion and addressing questions like the following:

- How did this discipline come into being?
- How and why is this discipline organized into major categories and subcategories?

- What research methods are used to generate knowledge in this discipline?
- What constitutes good evidence in this discipline?
- What constitutes good discourse in this discipline?
- What are the various types of literature (monographs, journal articles, gray literature, etc.) best accepted in this discipline?
- What are the alternate ways in which this discipline has been conceptualized, and who are its radical voices?
- What are ways in which newer information forms, as seen in Web 2.0, are influencing the knowledge base of this discipline?

In other words, an information-literate person needs to have a grasp of the sources and nature of whatever information is being addressed so that he or she can move comfortably within it while at the same time being aware of its biases.

One of the most serious gaps in our lack of good instruction in research processes today is simply our failure to help students understand the information base they have to deal with. The number of students who come to me with a list of journal ISSNs alone and expect that I can use ISSNs to help them find a particular article tells me that, not only do they not understand citation, but they do not understand the epistemology surrounding journal literature – how such material is produced, structured and disseminated. This lack of knowledge is both widespread and tragic if we, indeed, believe we are educating our students.

Once graduates reach the workplace, they will find themselves in new environments, and they will need to know how to navigate within the specific knowledge bases and belief systems of the organizations they work in (Mutch, 1999; Council of Europe, Council for Cultural Co-operation,

Culture Committee, 2000). The practice of looking closely at cultural context when discussing information and its structures should help university students to develop skills in discerning the historical factors, biases and concerns that result in the knowledge base within any setting.

Kane, Berryman, Goslin, and Meltzer (1990) argued that the detachment of "symbolic activities" from a "meaningful context" results in students writing to the rules rather than grasping the meaning of the projects they are working on. Without understanding the nature of information in real-life situations (such as grasping how academic literature is produced and what it is intended to do), students just follow the instructions for their "research" without really appreciating the nature of the sources they are using.

Markless and Streatfield (2007) have noticed an encouraging recent trend in the teaching of research, away from learning how to use libraries and toward enhancement of student information skills in a context of learning. This kind of understanding of information within disciplines and ultimately the workplace is crucial to the creation of skilled student researchers.

Ability to identify problems and acquire the information to solve them

Jones, Hoffman and National Center for Education Statistics's (1995) study of abilities needed by college graduates found that the faculty, employers and policymakers questioned agreed that a significant skill set

> involves the formulation of a plan for locating information, the combination of disparate pieces of information, determination of sufficient evidence to form a conclusion, and the judgment of what

background information would be useful. Equally important was the capacity to develop alternatives and hypotheses. (ibid., p. 162)

This entails the ability to formulate good problem statements and know where to go to find answers. It also requires strong search skills within complex databases in order to acquire narrowly defined information. As well, it demands critical evaluation even at the search level to discern schools of thought on the issue and determine levels of scholarship in the sources retrieved.

The SCONUL Seven Pillars of Information Literacy model in the UK (SCONUL Working Group on Information Literacy, 2011) provides a succinct list of requisite skills and knowledge:

IDENTIFY – Able to identify a personal need for information

SCOPE – Can assess current knowledge and identify gaps

PLAN – Can construct strategies for locating information and data

GATHER – Can locate and access the information and data they need

EVALUATE – Can review the research process and compare and evaluate information and data

MANAGE – Can organize information professionally and ethically

PRESENT – Can apply the knowledge gained: presenting the results of their research, synthesizing new and old information and data to create new knowledge and disseminating it in a variety of ways.

Weetman's (2005) study of close to 500 faculty members found that most of them rated an earlier and similar version of these skills at a value of 90 percent or better with regard to their own instructional goals. The seven skills may, therefore, be seen as highly congruent with higher education missions as well as embodying most of the purposes of student research.

One of the greatest struggles identified among students in higher education is simply that of being able to narrow a topic and formulate a problem statement. A significant barrier in this regard is that their earlier education has taught students that research is a task of compilation by which you gather data in order to synthesize it and then write *about* a topic. Moving them away from this "information as a goal" concept to an "information as a tool" view can be difficult. Students need to see research as a problem-solving exercise in which gathered information becomes a *means* to solve the problem rather than an end in itself. Only with considerable practice and professorial guidance can students become skilled at formulating concise and useful research questions or thesis statements.

Significant technological knowledge

No one can escape it these days: If you want to do most sorts of informational research, you will need to deal with technology – websites, databases and so on. This is where the ICT literacy movement, a version of information literacy that focuses on technology, can help. The Educational Testing Service, working with a number of colleges and universities comprising a quarter of US university students, has created The National Higher Education Information and Communication Technology (ICT) Initiative. Its definition of ICT Proficiency is as follows:

> ICT proficiency is the ability to use digital technology, communication tools, and/or networks appropriately to solve information problems in order to function in an information society. This includes the ability to use technology as a tool to research, organize, evaluate, and communicate information and the possession of a fundamental understanding of the ethical/legal issues surrounding the access and use of information. (Educational Testing Service, 2006, p. 11)

There is definitely a caution here, pointed out some time ago by Horton (1983), to the effect that computer literacy is not equivalent to information literacy, but the latter is an add-on to the former. While we must resist the common erroneous belief that developing proficiency with technology is equivalent to becoming information literate, there is no denying that proficiency with technology is foundational to any information literacy that is going to remain current and relevant. The Education Testing Service's study goes on to state: "While the ability to use particular digital devices, software, and infrastructure is important, technical know-how by itself is inadequate; individuals must possess the cognitive skills needed to identify and address various information needs and problems" (ibid., p. 12).

UNESCO has been a leader in enhancing technological skills and media literacy, even as it has been a strong partner of the worldwide information literacy movement. A set of workshops looking at UNESCO's work in information literacy concluded: "UNESCO needs to more closely link its Information Literacy and Media Literacy initiatives because the goals and purposes of both could be greatly enhanced if they were viewed as mutually supportive, complementary paradigms, not competing ones" (Boekhorst and Horton, 2009).

Thus, both technology and media have strong roles to play in information literacy, though it must be emphasized that technology and media skills are only a small step along the information literacy pathway.

Critical thinking and evaluation ability

In a 1995 study involving 600 faculty, employers and policymakers, respondents were asked to determine the writing, speaking, listening and critical skills required by college graduates (Jones, Hoffman, and National Center for Education Statistics, 1995). Findings showed that, with regard to critical thinking, students need to interpret and classify information, showing both ability to translate what they are reading into new environments and awareness of bias and inconsistencies. Thus understanding and critical evaluation were valued and viewed as necessary abilities in college graduates. Further, Jones and Hoffman reported high faculty ratings for student ability to evaluate evidence for quality and sufficiency, to make good inferences from the evidence, and to use evidence well in problem-solving.

The study does point out, however, that investigated faculty syllabi showed a professorial tendency to focus instruction on knowledge acquisition and application rather than on the skills of analysis and critical thinking. While educators want their students to think critically, they are often at a loss as to how to develop this facility in those whom they are teaching. Information literacy instruction, on the other hand, is far less concerned about knowledge-building than about enabling students to evaluate information critically. Thus it forms a missing piece in our students' education.

Keeping the goal consistent with higher education's mission

Hodge (2007) has posited the "student as scholar" model for higher education, with a focus on learning rather than on teaching. In essence, students learn to share the understandings and skills of their professors by doing research through the curriculum. Hodge's view is not particularly radical within a higher education that is moving (slowly to be sure) in the direction of a constructivist approach that puts learning more in the hands of students. He argues that "developing skills to find, critically evaluate, analyze, and synthesize information" is foundational to such an approach (ibid., p. 9).

On a broader scale, Cronon argued that it is the goal of liberal education to "nurture the growth of human talent in the service of human freedom" (1998, p. 74). Cronon's statement of outcomes needed in students – listening and hearing; reading and understanding; ability to talk with anyone; writing clearly, persuasively and movingly; ability to solve a "wide variety of puzzles and problems;" respecting rigor as a way of seeking truth; practicing "humility, tolerance and self-criticism;" understanding how to "get things done in the world," and nurturing and empowering others – would likely be on the lists of most higher educators. Cronon adds one more, the ability to "connect," that is, "being able to see connections that allow one to make sense of the world and act within it in creative ways" (ibid., p. 78).

Viewing Cronon's goals, we can see that information literacy weaves in and out them in perfect congruence. A student has to understand the nature of information sources available, know how to state problem questions clearly, have the ability to find the right information for the need and then to evaluate it well, on the way to using it effectively and ethically in order to "connect."

A related concept to "connecting" is that of "reflection," which is akin to critical thinking but emphasizes continuous evaluation and rethinking throughout the research process. Hughes, Bruce, and Edwards (2007) argue that such reflection should not be relegated to the evaluation of resources once they are found but should be a characteristic mindset while research is being conducted. "In other words, it underpins an active metacognitive approach to information literacy that encompasses critical analysis and evaluation as well as digital capabilities and information seeking processes" (ibid., p. 68).

The Partnership for 21st Century Learning Skills (2009) has expressed the goals of education this way: "Citizens of the 21st century need to think critically and creatively, embrace diversity and ambiguity, and create as well as consume information. They need to be resourceful and self-reliant, while also skilled at collaboration and group process." Information literacy is at the core of such aspirations.

We are thus, in discussing information literacy (ability within research processes), not looking for something alien from higher education's commonly stated goals for university students. Information and its use are integral to the mission of higher education, whether that mission should include critical thinking or analytical appropriation of sources or, indeed, creativity. The ability to do skilled information research is foundational to a good education. An information-literate student should be able to navigate with much greater facility within academic programs than a student who is information-illiterate.

What are we looking for?

Information literacy is a difficult concept for most academics. How can one speak intelligently about information itself as a topic of discussion? Information is an abstraction that appears impossibly vague, only really making sense when we are speaking about actual content.

Yet, as we have seen, the abstract idea of information does indeed need to be addressed, though it can find concrete form within actual subject disciplines. Where does the information vital to your discipline come from? Who produces it? Under what circumstances? With what kinds of evidence and discourse? In which vehicles of publication? These are questions of crucial importance to our students.

More than grasping the epistemology of information, students need to become adept at both understanding and handling the particular information in their field(s) of study. Whether this be the "student as scholar" model in which students learn the research patterns of their professors (Hodge, 2007), or some other approach, several of which will be suggested later in this book, in the end, students need to become competent handlers of information. Research processes can be taught, and students can become proficient handlers of information.

An image that comes to mind is that of the sports professional. A professional basketball player is not just someone who can dribble and pass and score. Such a player has taken the various elements of the game and woven them together into performance. It's not just a matter of skill but of knowledge, motivation, heart and fluid motion that shows profound integration of the elements of the sport. When a skilled player goes into action, there is seamless poetry in motion.

In the same way, an information literate student should be able to conceptualize a research problem, state it clearly, identify the nature and scope of information needed, find that information efficiently and effectively, evaluate it well, organize it, and apply it competently and ethically to the problem at hand. Such a student should use technology well and should have the ability to judge information for its worth, its "truth" value, and its applicability to whatever issue is under consideration.

We are speaking of competent information handlers, people who are not afraid of the massive amounts of information available to them, nor of the changing packages and technologies within which it is found. We are considering students who understand that, while they must master content, they also need to have a clear reading of the cultures and processes that form its context. Ultimately, we are seeking to create information sports stars.

The idea of research processes

"Research processes" represent the procedural side of the academic disciplines. Students, as we have seen, require a rigorous complex of understandings and skills in order to find success in their research. The study of and instruction in those understandings and skills form what we are calling ability in "research processes," equivalent to the technical term used by information professionals, "information literacy."

Is there actually a *need* to teach such processes? Surely students develop research skills on their own despite our early despair of their ever doing so? Some of them go on to graduate school and even become academics themselves. There must be a time when they finally "get it." The sad truth, as we shall see, is that such a time rarely comes unless we as educators ensure that our students are intentionally brought into the world of research processes.

2

Research ability inadequacies in higher education

Abstract: From pre-university, through undergraduate and graduate studies, even to the doctoral level, numerous studies have demonstrated significant gaps in student research ability. The notions that students become skilled at research simply by doing it (osmosis theory) or that their technological ability equates with research ability are not supported by studies investigating these issues. Students tend to overestimate their own abilities while demonstrating deficits when tested on those abilities. Even faculty members are struggling to keep up with technological change in research, and many of them appear to have limitations in their ability to teach technologically-based research skills to their students. Disturbingly, many in academia appear unaware that a significant problem has developed.

Key words: osmosis theory, overestimated ability, technological change.

I received an e-mail from a desperate graduate student at a major American university. Her plight did not surprise me. She wrote:

> I spend hours searching when I could be reading or analyzing or writing . . . I'm still trying to resolve this issue – (I'm too ashamed to tell my professor at _____) – here I'm in a LIS beginning course training for some

aspect of librarianship – and don't know how to use the searches efficiently! The tutorials are there on the website, but they are not user-friendly.

This was a graduate student working on her Master's degree in Library and Information Studies, yet she was struggling with understanding common academic research databases.

Another graduate student e-mailed me for some advice on a research project and later responded: "Thank you for your encouraging words on research being available online! I feel like I will be able to accomplish my research paper on servant leadership. It has been frustrating having little or no guidance over the years."

I received a telephone call from a 52-year-old woman finishing a bachelor's degree in a night program at an unspecified institution. She was taking a course for which the professor had asked the class to write an interdisciplinary research paper. In her estimation, while the professor had provided her with some rather broad examples of what could be done in such an assignment, he had made no real attempt to explain how actually to do it. Nor did she have any confidence that even he knew what the process might be, let alone how to explain it to the class. Her research skills were minimal, but no one at her institution had offered her any real help. Instead, when she wasn't phoning me for advice, she was reading and marking up a copy of my textbook, *Research Strategies: Finding Your Way through the Information Fog.*

As a reference librarian, I observe, on a daily basis, students who do not know the difference between a peer-reviewed journal article and a website, who have no idea how to determine the best places to look for information, and who lack the skills to evaluate the information they do find. While they have access to wonderfully sophisticated research databases, they treat them like Google, if they use them at all. In fact, when I discuss with them how they use Google itself, they admit to frustration, having little understanding of how best to formulate even simple searches in this ubiquitous search engine.

Today's university students in the main have little grasp of the world of information itself – where it comes from, under what conditions it is published, what types of information exist, what tools are available to help them discover it, how to use those tools, how to critically discern what is accurate/useful information, and how to apply information to the research task at hand. This is the subject matter of the research processes that will form the core of this book. Students are swimming in a sea of information, but they have little ability to harness it and use it well.

Librarians see the effects of the problem every day – students who don't know what a library catalog is or does, who don't know what to do with a call number, who think they can locate a journal article if they write down the ISSN of the journal it came from, who see no significant difference between a peer-reviewed journal article and a Wikipedia entry, who believe that all the world's knowledge can be found by Google alone, and who think that five references (only one of which was actually used) constitute an acceptable bibliography for a major research paper.

Where the problem starts

It's very common for university professors to lay the blame for the inadequate critical thinking and writing skills of their students on poor training in elementary and high schools. Such criticism is not entirely justified. For one thing, most pre-university students lack the mental maturity even to be able to perform sophisticated critical thought. For another, the leap to higher education has always been a huge one requiring a lot of catch-up. (That's why they call it "higher" education.)

There is evidence, as well, that pre-college educational institutions are looking for new ways to meet the demands of the information age. Culp et al. (2003) found that, in 20 years of study of the use of information technology in pre-college institutions, a fundamental shift had occurred, from seeing technology as a possibly useful adjunct to instruction, to viewing it as a "tool of *transformation*, which promised, simply by its presence and capabilities, to bring change to how teachers teach, how schools are organized, and how students work together and learn" (ibid., p. 20). The new emphasis on 21st Century Skills (Partnership for 21st Century Skills, 2009), and recent online curricula designed to promote information literacy (such as Scholastic's Expert Space: www.scholastic.com/expertspace) show promise for the future.

Unfortunately, the new emphasis on technology in learning, while generating great excitement, has not translated into widespread development of student information handling skills. McEuen pointed out that, while pre-college students are using technology widely even in their schools, college students in his qualitative study "reported that their high school experience encompassed the implementation of basic skills (e-mail, Internet browsing, and word processing) at best" (2001, p. 16). The extensive study by Flanagan, Metzger and Hartsell (2010) shows that children up to age 18 are more trusting of Internet sources than they should be. Development of information abilities to required pre-university levels, from gathering information to evaluating it, seems not to be on the agenda of many high school curricula.

Duke and Ward summarize the problem as follows: "All too often, teachers are merely presenters of ready-made information rather than facilitators of knowledge construction, and their students are passive consumers of other people's ideas rather than active participants in the co-construction of knowledge" (2009, p. 254).

Clearly, if the pre-college education system isn't embracing the more sophisticated tools of the modern information age, then any hope of instructing pre-college students in the nature of the new information environment, the technology needed to discover information, and the skills required to evaluate it properly, is doomed to fail.

This is not to criticize pre-university instruction as much as to say that, with the world having changed dramatically since 1989 (birth of the WWW), education is still grappling with how to get computers into student hands. We have not begun to address significantly the information skills of the pupil in today's classroom. Further, we have yet to understand the extent to which our information world has been changed by technology. Our pre-university students are ill-equipped with the information-handling skills needed to move into the workforce, let alone to meet the demands of college and university.[1]

Williams and Wavell (2007) found that, while there were some common points between secondary teachers' conceptions of information literacy and those found in information literacy literature, there were notable differences, leading to deficiencies. Using the language of information literacy, which we have chosen to describe as ability with "research processes," they write:

> Teachers generally thought of information literacy as process and skills oriented, including reading skills and basic understanding of text and vocabulary, rather than

> outcome oriented (i.e. knowledge building, creation, communication), with little emphasis on the relationship with learning or problem solving. (ibid., p. 209)

Beyond limitations in understanding the nature and complexity of information literacy (or "research processes"), an understanding that improved among the teachers involved as the study went on, Williams and Wavell found that most teachers believed the demands of the curriculum prevented them from helping their students become more skilled. In other words, content trumped process to such an extent that there was no room for development of research skills that would foster learning when their students entered higher education.

Is the complaint of university professors valid? Do incoming students lack the skills to do adequate research or even to handle information well? One of the largest studies of entering university students was done in Quebec, Canada (Mittermeyer and Quirion, 2003). It surveyed just over 3000 students, finding that less than 36 percent of them understood such research foundations as the characteristics of scholarly journals, the difference between library catalogs and bibliographic databases, search terminology constructions that would eliminate non-essential words, the use of controlled vocabularies in databases, identification of a journal citation, and issues regarding the ethical use of Internet information. The researchers concluded that "a significant number of students have a limited knowledge, or no knowledge, of basic elements characterizing the information research process."

Several other researchers have found the same. Kennedy et al. (2008) surveyed more than 2000 incoming Australian university students who demonstrated that, while they were highly technology-aware in using a core of tool types (computers, cell phones, e-mail), their knowledge of, and facility with, academic tools for research were limited. The researchers commented: "Moreover, it is recognized that core technology based skills do not necessarily translate into sophisticated skills with other technologies or general information literacy."

The *First Year Information Literacy in the Liberal Arts Assessment* (2008), studying students in several American and Canadian institutions, found for 2006 and 2007 that incoming university students had weak understanding of many foundational information handling and research skills (though this weakness was ameliorated when information literacy instruction was done). For example, less than half of new students understood the function of a Boolean "or" search, and most could not identify a citation to a journal article or a portion of a book. Only about half had used library catalogs and less than a quarter had used journal databases (though almost everyone used search engines).

We may, in fact, have created a misnomer in referring to our young people as the "Google Generation." The University College London (UCL) CIBER Group (2008) study, a combination of literature review and live study of information seeking, found that today's so-called Google Generation shows no uniformity in the use of technology for information seeking. Less than a third of UK teenagers have a deep interest in IT technology. Moreover, "there is no evidence in the serious literature that young people are expert searchers, nor that the search skills of young people has improved with time" (ibid., p. 22). Little effort was being devoted by these students to evaluating information for accuracy, quality or relevance.

The UCL study concludes:

> If the erratic behaviour we are seeing in digital libraries really is the result of failure at the library terminal, then society has a major problem. Information skills are

needed more than ever and at a higher level if people are to really avail themselves of the benefits of an information society. (ibid., p. 32)

More recently, the Ontario (Canada) Confederation of University Faculty Associations surveyed 2000 professors about their freshman students' skills and found deterioration, over earlier studies, in freshman ability to handle university studies (Ontario (Canada) Confederation of University Faculty Associations, 2009). Of the five most often stated deficits, two stand out: "Lack of required writing, mathematical and critical thinking skills" and "poor research skills as evidenced by an overreliance on Internet tools like Wikipedia as external research sources" (ibid., p. 2).

The British study, *Higher Education in a Web 2.0 World* (Melville, 2009) pointed out serious gaps in the information literacy of school age and university students. The top two fundamental issues the report identified as most needing to be addressed with urgency were the digital divide and information literacy. The study's conclusion: "Information literacies, including searching, retrieving, critically evaluating information from a range of appropriate sources and also attributing it – represent a significant and growing deficit area" (ibid., p. 6).

So the answer is generally, yes, the students who enter our colleges and universities as first year undergraduates are often poorly equipped to handle research and information tasks at the higher education level.

University students and information skills – an overview

True or false?: *College and university students over time develop reasonably good research skills simply through practice. Any students who do not are likely unmotivated or require remedial instruction.* Many professors I know would answer, "True." And they would be wrong. The research unequivocally tells us that the answer is "No." In fact, most students perpetuate both their lack of understanding of the information world and its tools and their assumption that there is little to learn about doing research. Students do not develop significantly better research skills by the experience of doing research. While they tend to overestimate their research ability, they go on performing at a level far lower than their programs of study expect of them.

Massey-Burzio's (1998) study of undergraduates at Johns Hopkins University (an institution with a strong emphasis on research writing) found that students continued to have trouble understanding how libraries are organized, tended to retrieve too much information and not know what to do with it, chose the wrong databases for the information they need, tended to stick to one or two favorite databases, and much preferred searching for books to finding journal articles. Her telling conclusion is that "library patrons think that using a library does not require all that much skill development and knowledge, . . . [and] they are, therefore, unwilling to invest time and energy into developing those skills and knowledge" (ibid., p. 215).

This unwillingness of students to recognize the need for skill development is often seen in the literature. Andretta et al. (2008), for example, found that most students view information literacy instruction as a waste of time, assuming that they know everything because they are technologically literate.

The technological abilities of today's students seem to offer little help when it comes to doing academic research. McEuen (2001) reported on a study within the Association of Colleges of the South that found that students had strong self-reported skills in technology use. But when it came to "using a database system to set up and access useful information" (ibid., p. 14), the self-reported scores went down dramatically, with only 31.4 percent of students believing they had average to expert skills (see also Lippincott, 2005).

The supposed positive relationship between developing technological ability and research process skills is increasingly being debunked as an optimistic but unfounded assumption. Katz and Macklin (2007) show strong evidence that frequency of student use of information technology does not correlate with information technology skills. Katz (2007) discussed the release of preliminary research from the Educational Testing Service (ETS) showing that "while students may be tech savvy when it comes to entertainment, they may not have the critical thinking skills to perform the kinds of information management and research tasks necessary for academic success." Using a measure of ICT (Information and Communications Technology) Literacy, which is akin to information literacy, ETS found that only 44 percent of students could identify a research statement that met the demands of an assignment. Only 35 percent correctly narrowed a topic. In a database search only 50 percent used a strategy that minimized irrelevant results.

Alexius Macklin, Associate Professor of Library Science at Purdue University, added this comment in Katz's report:

> The preliminary research from ETS shows us that a majority of our students are not ICT literate enough to succeed academically . . . they do not currently have the skills to analyze and synthesize information into something manageable and useful for their needs.

Overall, on tests of these skills, students earned about half of the points they should have (Educational Testing Service, 2006).

Pan et al. (2007) found that college students are more influenced by the position of results in a list than perceived relevance of results for the research being done. That could well mean that they are more likely to choose the early results of a search engine or database search, rather than sifting through results to glean the most useful information.

Students seem unable to understand how the world of academic information functions, and for good reason. Jill Jenson, an associate professor at University of Minnesota, explains:

> How can our students reasonably be expected to know the difference between a weekly magazine such as *U.S. News* and a scholarly publication such as the *Journal of the American Dietetic Association* if their experience with either is exclusively online, where each "page" looks the same? (2004, p. 208)

The picture is no better when it comes to higher level skills such as effective evaluation and use of sources. Wang and Artero (2005), in a study of Internet use among 647 students, found that 40 percent believed that information found through an Internet search engine was as reliable as that in books and journals, while a further 33 percent were undecided on the issue. Though 78 percent reported that they evaluated Web resources before using them, 58 percent indicated that they would use a piece of information so long as it fitted their point of view. The authors concluded that their subjects were creating their own highly subjective evaluation criteria. "Although the students in this study judged that they had critically evaluated Web information, their responses to the survey questions showed that they were not equipped with sufficient knowledge and skills to critically evaluate Web resources" (ibid., p. 80).

It has been overwhelmingly demonstrated in multiple studies that students continue to struggle, year after year, to meet the research project demands of their professors. Head and Eisenburg (2009), in an investigation of 86 second year to senior undergraduates at several American universities, found significant levels of frustration with research. Though most students had developed personal procedures to complete research projects, it was often at the cost of wasted time and poor results. Head and Eisenburg concluded:

> In general, students reported being challenged, confused, and frustrated by the research process, despite the convenience, relative ease, or ubiquity of the Internet . . . Participants also reported having particular difficulty traversing a vast and ever-changing information landscape . . . Overall, we conclude that students are challenged and often inexperienced with "finding context"—a requisite for conducting course-related research and to a lesser extent, everyday life research. (ibid., p. 13)

Take note that the subjects of this study were not first year students. Their experience of research processes seems to have done little to improve either their skills or their understanding of those processes.

Information literacy of senior undergraduate/graduate students

It is a well-accepted element of academic mythology that undergraduates may begin their studies with gaps in research ability but their skills become more fully developed as they complete their assignments (the "information literacy by osmosis" myth). While students do, inevitably, become somewhat more skilled as time goes on, the notion that they are competent researchers by the time they reach their senior undergraduate year has been soundly refuted by a significant number of studies.

Knight-Davis and Sung (2008) investigated 957 undergraduate writing samples from electronic writing portfolios at Eastern Illinois University. While the number of papers even having reference lists rose from 39 percent to 51 percent over the four papers submitted per student, the number of citations did not. Fewer than 10 percent of the papers that did have reference lists had more than 10 citations in them.

Weetman (2005) specifically studied the "osmosis theory" in a survey of faculty at De Montfort University, UK. Among those faculty who responded, fully 93 percent believed that students should have achieved recognized standards of information literacy by the time they had completed their undergraduate studies. The study concludes:

> Despite this recognition of the value of information literacy skills, it has also been shown that there is very little activity, on the part of academic staff, in order to either teach or assess information skills or even develop them through student-centered learning. This is most noticeable within the context of . . . the ability to locate and access information – which is highly valued by academic staff but is the least taught. (ibid., p. 459)

Maughan (2001) presented surveys administered to senior undergraduates at the University of California-Berkeley in 1994, 1995, and 1999 which showed that students consistently overestimated their research ability, while, of eight discipline-specific groups of students studied, five showed failing scores even on measures of lower-order information literacy. His study concluded: "students think they know more about accessing information and conducting library research than they are able to demonstrate when put to the test" (ibid., p. 83).

Not only are these students not developing library skills, but they are also deficient in assessing the information they do find. Kuh and Gonyea (2003) studied data gathered from over 300,000 participants in the College Student Experiences Questionnaire, 1984–2002. While more students were using databases in the later years, almost 20 percent of senior students indicated that they never make judgments about the quality of information they acquire for academic work. The researchers concluded: "This is an unacceptably high number of students about to graduate from college who, by their own report, are underprepared to live and work in an information-rich world" (ibid., p. 266).

Alison Head's (2007) research may seem a bit more encouraging, in that her study of upper level undergraduate students found them reducing their use of Google as a first choice when starting research, in preference to course readings and even library resources. But her results are telling nevertheless as she argues that: "Most students were confused by what college-level research entails." About 60 percent of her subjects struggled with narrowing topics and making them manageable, while the same percentage admitted being overwhelmed by the number of resources available to them. Interestingly, the greatest frustration was reserved for the perceived lack of guidance from professors regarding the conduct of quality research (supported by an actual lack of helpful instruction in assignment handouts studied). We may thus assume that these students will graduate having received less than complete guidance from their professors and lacking research skills they should have had.[2] Clearly there is a disconnection between what professors think they are communicating and what their students are actually able to understand.

Head's (2008) study of junior and senior undergraduates in the humanities and social sciences found ongoing struggles with the research process:

> Most students are baffled by college level research, especially when they just begin the process and define their information needs . . . Other challenges relate to accessing and critically evaluating quality resources, especially what students describe as their own inability to narrow down topics and make them manageable. Students also have a tendency to become overwhelmed by the plethora of available resources, including many from the Web, that are available to them . . . The most significant obstacle for students, however, is figuring out what each research assignment entails, especially when they are writing different papers for more than one professor. (ibid., p. 437)

A complicating study is that of Rosenblatt (2010), who found that upper level undergraduates were indeed able to meet the bibliographic requirements of their professors but were not able to synthesize gathered resources into the bodies of their research papers. Yet, when we look more closely at the nature of those "bibliographic requirements," we find that expectations of the cooperating professor were low (three articles, one book and one presentation text). Presumably most students could keyword search specified databases and obtain the five resources required. This low level of expectation, however, simply highlights the fact that a number of professors have come to believe that their students are only capable of doing minimal work in compiling bibliographies. Thus the professorial requirements are minimal as well.

Paradoxically, considering the frustrations they experience, it is a well-documented phenomenon that students consistently overestimate their own research ability. For example, Massey-Burzio's (1998) study found significant discrepancies between high self-perceptions of students at Johns Hopkins University and their extensive ignorance of actual research skills. Ren (2000) found that the positive views of students regarding their perceived research ability had no significant relationship with their actual self-efficacy unless they received research training. This adds support to the earlier study of Fischoff (1986) who demonstrated that, while overconfidence regarding research ability is the norm among students, it increases in proportion to their lack of actual knowledge of the research process.

If we view yesterday's senior undergraduate as tomorrow's new graduate student, we can see a continuum in the information literacy problem in grad schools. Graduate students also overestimate their abilities while showing significant gaps in their information discovery and handling facility. Many participants in a 2003 study of 330 beginning graduate law students believed that their research skills were well advanced, while they failed dramatically in an actual test of skills (Anon, 2004). Perrett (2004) found that 81 percent of incoming graduate students in several disciplines required further information literacy instruction in order to meet educational standards, though many of them had self-rated their skills as good or excellent.

Such results are no surprise to university reference librarians who regularly observe significant gaps between personal assessment and actual skills, from freshman to grad school levels. Kuruppu and Gruber (2006) as well as Gallacher (2007) have found evidence of the same overestimation of ability even in more advanced graduate students and faculty.

Gross and Latham (2009) point to the field of competency theory as a possible explanation. Competency theory, as discussed by Kruger and Dunning (1999) and Ehrlinger et al. (2008) demonstrates that the less competent someone is at a skill, the more likely he or she is to overestimate their ability. It is also the case that the less competent will generally not learn how better to estimate ability from further trial and error. Lack of skill, in fact, leads directly to inability to discern lack of skill. Thus the confidence of students who believe they already know how to do research is not at all incongruent with their less than adequate skills when actually tested.

In the face of growing use of Internet search engines by students, research is consistently demonstrating that 45 percent or more of students, even graduate students right to the doctoral level, use search engines such as Google and Google Scholar as their predominant search tools in research (for example, Griffiths and Brophy, 2005; Liu and Yang, 2004, p. 26; University College London (UCL) CIBER Group, 2008). This demands that we question further whether or not students do well searching even with Google. Evidence is available, once again, to show that they do not (Griffiths and Brophy, 2005).

Graduate students in carrying out their research projects tend to reveal a strong level of uncertainty. George et al. (2006) studied the information-seeking behaviors of 100 graduate students from a wide range of disciplines. One interesting finding was the extent to which students initially sought the advice of professors and peers on the best way to begin research projects. Professors often responded with suggested authors or particular approaches students might take. About 40 percent of students sought out librarians for help with search strategies and shaping their topics.

Most of these students used the World Wide Web as a significant tool for information seeking, though less than half saw themselves as specifically searching for scholarly papers and articles as opposed to more general websites. The students expressed personal challenges with information overload, search strategy and evaluation of resources. Many pursued a pattern of following up on citations in materials they located (citation chaining), though this method, while useful, does not ensure comprehensiveness.

The same study revealed that 42 percent of graduate students reported that a lack of knowledge of tools and resources, along with a skills gap in using them effectively, was limiting their research success. From previous studies demonstrating that upper level students consistently overestimate their research ability, the self-declared 42 percent may be much higher in practice. The strong use of basic Internet search engines, despite their uneven results, is another indicator that convenience and searching ease are trumping search sophistication, such as we find in library databases.

The information literacy gap appears to exist across graduate disciplines. A telling study by Randall, Smith, Clark and Foster (2008) demonstrates haphazard, confused and inconsistent research methods among students doing doctoral research across a number of disciplines. Other than the mining of existing bibliographies, it appears that none of those subjects had genuinely sophisticated skills in locating information. Few of them were using bibliographic managers to organize their resources, and there seemed to be a general air of trial and error in all of their research methods.

Gallacher (2007) reported widespread inadequacies of research ability in studies of incoming law students in seven institutions and saw little evidence that the research training available to law students was succeeding. His conclusion:

> Taken together, the studies present a potentially discouraging picture: while incoming law students are clearly intelligent and capable, and have excelled academically at every previous stage of their education, the available data suggest that many incoming students have information literacy deficits that will affect them through their career in law school and on into the practice of law, and that they are unaware that such deficits exist. (ibid., p. 32)

The LexisNexis International Workplace Productivity Survey (2010) reserved a portion of its study for lawyers worldwide. Six of ten such lawyers agreed that the quality of their work is at times impaired by the sheer volume of information they encounter daily. If they lack the information handling skills they need, the problem is surely going to be exacerbated.[3]

Lippincott and Kuchida (2005) found that MBA graduates continue to struggle with information needs in the business world. "Of concern was the lack of differentiation between information skills and technological abilities and the lack of understanding of the complex nature of information used to make important business decisions."

Brown (2005), studying molecular biology graduate students, determined that, while they were reading a selection of key journals on a regular basis, these students relied on bioinformatics databases much more than they did on key journal databases. Approximately half of those surveyed in this study were not users of common databases for scientific information, such as SciFinder Scholar, Web of Science, Biological Abstracts, and Zoological Record.

The information literacy of faculty members

The world of information has changed dramatically in the past twenty years, and so have the now highly technological tools of research. Faculty members, busy with their own disciplines and tending to keep up with advances in their field primarily by reading specific journals and maintaining a strong network of colleagues, often find that the ever-changing tools of research are leaving them behind. When academics actually need to do literature reviews, it may well be that the complexities, and downright strangeness, of the databases they have to use prove to be a barrier. Many of them, particularly in the sciences, are turning to Google Scholar, which, though seemingly easy to use, has a simplistic search interface and confusing result displays.

Over the past while, I have had a number of professors come to me for private (and I do mean "private") sessions to help them through their research tasks. They are generally uncomfortable and embarrassed, but they also reveal a level of anxiety in the midst of their attempted bravado ("I should know this, but I've been so busy lately; when will they stop changing these databases every year?" and so on). While academic faculty members are frustrated with the shoddy research done by students (Gilchrist, 2007), they often fail to see that the winds of their own research requirements have changed and their ship is listing badly.

Massey-Burzio (1998) found that, while a number of faculty members studied at Johns Hopkins University admitted that they lacked certain research skills, they did not see the problem as sufficient to pursue further. Could this be in part because of embarrassment about admitting that they have not kept up with technology? There is, in fact, a degree of professorial resistance to upgrading their own research skills. Feldman and Sciammarella (2000), for example, found that only 35 percent of 425 faculty members at the City University of New York had attended their own library's seminars on technological resources for research.

Hall (1999) describes the introduction of a well-received faculty upgrading program. From her experience with the program, she comments about faculty:

> They are quite familiar with the literature in their fields and they regularly look at their journals, but many have not kept up with the changes that technology has imposed on information dissemination in their disciplines. This is a disservice to their students who are being given tired, old, and inappropriate assignments that are geared toward print access.

More professors now appear to be waking up to the onward march of technology, and academic librarians regularly find themselves providing upgrading to those faculty members willing to admit to inadequacies in their skills with research technology. Meanwhile, however, many students are still being given assignments that fail to recognize the power of the newer research tools.

Shen (2007) surveyed social science professors at the University of Wisconsin-Madison. While a number of them were making use of electronic resources, there was high reliance on Google and free databases on the Internet. In their use of all databases, these academics expressed struggles with doing the difficult task of computer searching, viewing their search engines as not intelligent enough to provide what was being sought except through a lot of brainstorming and guesswork.

Stoan (1991) sought, decades ago, to provide a corrective to the consensus view of librarians that most academics seem to rely more on personal networks and citation gleaning than on databases. While professional academics appear haphazard in their research methodology, each of them is part of an environment in which skills and expertise are furthered by a network of collaboration and reliance on key publications. The fact, argued Stoan, that good products come out of their research shows that it is effective. Bibliographic tools, in fact (fairly primitive when Stoan was writing) produce inconsistent results, and most academics rarely need to produce a full literature review from scratch.

All of Stoan's arguments remain true today, yet they fail to address the issue that, while immersed in their world of current journal issues and academic collaboration, today's average faculty members seem unable or unwilling to impart a knowledge of sophisticated bibliographic tools to their students. These students, lacking a professional skill and knowledge base themselves, absolutely must rely on bibliographic tools even if their professors do not. And when faculty members need to expand their scope by using the same tools, they often lack the advanced skills to optimize their searches.

A study entitled *Higher Education in a Web 2.0 World* concludes with a statement regarding university professors:

> With the pace of development in web-based sources of information, it would be naïve to assume that staff will possess the range of skills necessary to navigate and exploit them. Inevitably, they too will have support needs if their skills are to remain current. We believe these must not be overlooked. (Melville, 2009, p. 35)

The bottom line: information illiteracy in academia

Admittedly, students never were very adept at handling information and doing research. Professors for decade upon decade have been well used to getting slap-dash, mediocre research papers showing limited analytical thinking and sporting too few references. But the rise of information technology has added complex new wrinkles to the problem.

Many of today's students go first to Google or Wikipedia for most any kind of research project (Head and Eisenberg, 2009), the latter being a tool that a goodly number of their professors warn them against using. But students do not care, because they know that Wikipedia is where the information is. Students will use books in their research, if they can find them, but rarely journals. Student search skills, despite the seemingly technologically advanced nature of today's young people, are poor to dismal, whether using Google or a proprietary journal database.

But this only scratches the surface of the problem. As Jenson (2004) has made plain, the web-based nature of most students' research experience turns the notion of such things as journal volumes, issue numbers, and dates into something quite alien. The average undergraduate cannot distinguish, from their citations, the difference between a journal article and an essay in a book. Students, addressing most research information electronically, see it as content rather than understanding it as a collection of distinct entities like books, journals, and so on.

Clearly, many students, whether undergraduate or graduate, have trouble formulating research questions/thesis statements, identifying their information needs, locating relevant information by use of good search strategies, evaluating the information they've found, and applying it effectively to the research problem at hand. This is what we mean by ability with research processes. Its missing presence in student curricula is both mystifying and disturbing.

Perhaps even more seriously, faculty members as a whole, as we will see, do not appear to have noticed the gap, nor do they have either the strategies or, apparently, the time to do much to improve the research abilities of their students. In fact, a significant proportion of professors themselves are rapidly becoming less able to do their own research, because the skills required to handle today's information environment are radically different from what they were even 15 or 20 years ago.

The world of information has changed in ways that we are only beginning to appreciate. Sadly (and dangerously), at the very moment in which the information age has finally arrived, those who would best be able to walk into that world, skilled and confident, are finding themselves ill-equipped, and their teachers often unable to provide them with the abilities they need.

Notes

1. Badke (2009a) considers possible ways high schools could inject more information literacy into their curricula.
2. See Head and Eisenberg's YouTube video summarizing actual student frustrations, particularly with formulating research questions, understanding what is expected of them, and finding relevant information: *http://www.youtube.com/ watch?v=rmEzo51e_SQandfeature=related.*
3. This author was recently approached by a lawyer with decades of experience who admitted significant gaps in his own research ability and asked for help.

3

Research processes and faculty understanding

Abstract: The teaching of research processes has not been given priority in academic institutions. Reasons for this include a misunderstanding among both students and professors of the learning task demanded; a lack of support from academic administrators; the fact that the major literature on research processes instruction resides in the library literature rather than in the higher education literature; false notions that students learn research processes on their own and that the new technologies make students more able to accomplish good research; faculty culture that puts more stress on content than process; a lack of regard in academia for the contribution that academic librarians can make; and a lack of clear direction from agencies that set educational standards. In essence, the teaching of research processes is not a priority because so few people recognize that there is a problem to address.

Key words: academic administrators, faculty culture, library literature, osmosis, technology.

While "information literacy" (the technical term for ability with research processes) may be an expression commonly used in library literature, it certainly has not been given a high priority generally in university programs. The Primary Research Group (2008) surveyed over 100 colleges and universities in Canada and the United States on the degree to which they had implemented information literacy instruction within their curricula. The study's findings support the common perception that the vast percentage of information literacy instruction is done through single sessions, generally lasting an hour or less. Fewer than 6 percent of respondents had a one- or two-credit course in information literacy required for graduation in their institutions and fewer than 4 percent had such a course at the three-credit level. About 25 percent had an information literacy component built into basic writing and composition classes.

When it came to any form of information literacy instruction required for graduation, the results were still less than 30 percent of all institutions surveyed. Only about 21 percent of respondents gave an information/computer literacy test that was required for graduation. Over half of respondents had no information literacy graduation requirement of any kind. Most respondents foresaw little progress in making information literacy a priority in the coming three years.

So, with the massive spread of new knowledge technologies making ability with information an even more imperative skill, why do most universities still relegate it to the level of brief remedial treatment? Why do accrediting bodies for the most part give it only lip service, if they mention it at all? This chapter will address the reasons for this lack of serious consideration given to teaching research processes.

The understanding gap

To describe the most common method for research processes instruction within the majority of universities, we would have to use the term "short-term remedial." Hosts of academic librarians perform single one-hour sessions (colloquially referred to as "one-shots") of library orientation that are either generic or subject-specific, the latter often related to upcoming assignments. Librarians explain to students what they should know how to do, and sometimes those students get a chance to practice their basic skills. Any notion of sophisticated, comprehensive education is precluded, much as it would be if you were assuming that your adolescent son or daughter was competent to drive an automobile after 40 minutes of explanation and 15 minutes of practice.

Though we are dealing, in the teaching of research processes, with a complex and challenging set of understandings and skills that require much instruction and practice to develop to the point of sophistication, the response of academia to this point has been to make it a remedial issue. This indicates a misunderstanding of the nature of the challenge and, indeed, of the complexity of research processes.

Even librarians, who regularly see the great gap in information literacy exhibited by most university students, have been slow to acknowledge the full scope of what is required in teaching research processes. They have been so used to teaching people how to use libraries (thus thinking of information literacy "library instruction") that they have failed to grasp that library instruction *per se* is not the point.

Information literacy is about *understanding information and how it works*. It is about introducing students to the forms of information available to them, and then helping them determine the nature of the information they need for any specific context, how to find it, how to evaluate it, and how to use it effectively and ethically. To equate this with teaching students how to use a library is as short-sighted as assuming that driving a car simply requires that a person needs to know how to use a steering wheel.

To illustrate, imagine that a student wants to do research on the effect of the world economic crisis of 2008+ on federal government regulation of American banking. A library instruction approach would point the student to the library catalog (perhaps with some suggestions for subject headings), to the journal databases and perhaps to government documents. The student, bewildered by the alien world of academic and professional information in general, would then muddle through "research," never really understanding what she or he was dealing with.

An information literacy (research processes) approach would begin by guiding the student to formulate the research goal clearly. For example, the student might create a question such as this: "To what extent was the US government negligent in not preventing the economic crisis of 2008+?" Armed with a clear goal, the information literacy instructor would then help the student to assess the various information sources that might provide good material.

Books for this topic might be of some value, but the short time lag between events and studied commentary on them may limit the number of useful titles. Journals would be a good choice, but what kinds of journals in what subject areas? The student would need guidance regarding the best ways to adapt journal database searches to the problem being addressed (rather than just learning the various search features). Further, for this topic, the Google-searchable Internet is liable to be full of contradictory unsubstantiated opinion on this topic, but various government websites and Google searches for updated banking regulations might be more useful. Best would be incisive analysis by independent financial experts who have no particular biases to support. An information literacy approach indeed might not even in every case take the student to a library as such.

To assume that we can meet all the needs demanded by research processes with a library tour or an hour of instruction is to misunderstand utterly what those needs are. Research instruction is not a remedial topic but a whole way of thinking about information and its use. To miss this point is to relegate student skill and understanding to the back burner.

Students themselves, unfortunately, tend to believe that there is little to be learned in order to become adept at research processes. As Head and Eisenberg put it:

> Students conceptualize research, especially tasks associated with seeking information, as a competency learned by rote, rather than as an opportunity to learn, develop, or expand upon an information-gathering strategy which leverages the wide range of resources available to them in the digital age. (2009, p. 1)

The challenge of developing skilled student researchers is thus a complex one, demanding that they acquire knowledge of information typology, problem identification, and research methods, as well as information acquisition, evaluation and effective application. The historical connection between bibliographic instruction (library instruction) and information literacy has unfortunately led to the situation in which those who attempt to teach research processes are predominantly given only one or two hours with students to accomplish their instructional goals, as if an introduction to the library were sufficient.

This creates a damaging circular argument – if teaching research skills is primarily done through one-shot sessions, then it must be a remedial task and easily accomplished within the time allotted, otherwise more time would be devoted to it. But, because we devote so little time to it, the assumption of faculty is that the one-shot instruction pattern is sufficient and that little more can be done to improve student abilities through further education. Faculty hear our technical term "information literacy" and assume a short orientation period that teaches students how to use a library and search databases (Webber and Johnston, 2006; Andretta et al., 2008). The result is just what faculty members currently believe – students normally do just muddle through their research and perform with minimal skill. Nothing more, apparently, can be expected, though some improvement will surely come (we hope, though with no real evidence to support it) as students gain more experience.

The reality is that genuine research process abilities are developed by students by the same means that many other knowledge-based skills develop – from a combination of instruction and practice over a significant period of time. The teaching of research processes is a challenging discipline involving effort closer to learning a new language than to learning how to read a spreadsheet. Yet it is both possible and feasible, if we work at it, to develop student research skills to a significant level, something that few academics seem currently to believe, having not experienced it in person.

Thus, a crucial reason why research instruction does not have a significant place in academia is the fact that it is misunderstood and underestimated. If there are few opportunities to watch students become skilled researchers, academics will assume that it cannot be done, that students just do not do research well and cannot be taught how to handle information skillfully except perhaps at the graduate level. And, since most students complete their programs of study anyway, even without sophisticated information skills, we assume that somehow they have turned out all right.

The university administration gap

Webber and Johnston (2006), in a British study of key stakeholders within universities, found minimal understanding of information literacy among academic administrators. While there was some discussion about information skills, administrators confused information literacy with computer literacy. "Information literacy" as a term did not appear in university documents, and it found no place in marketing the university. When dealing with the library, administrators were more interested in holdings and in quantification of transactions (how many books were borrowed, etc.) than the education of users. No administrative committee in the Webber and Johnston study believed that its mandate included fostering research processes ability.

Thus, even if librarians or faculty members were to propose a research processes instruction program, the possibility of getting such a program into the realm of approval and funding would be limited. The concept represented by terminology like "information literacy" or even "ability with research processes," fuzzy to many faculty, appears alien to most university administrators. This problem is echoed by policymakers in society in general. A European workshop on information literacy ("Conclusions and Recommendations to UNESCO and CEI," 2006) concluded:

> One of the main reasons for not addressing the Information Literacy problem is the insufficient understanding of the concept and its relevance to today's information society and knowledge-based economies among policy makers, information professionals, private sector representatives and general public.

The silo problem

In the summer of 2008, I made a list of the 32 most highly regarded journals related to higher education teaching and administration, searching their contents as far back as possible for the term "information literacy." The results were astounding. Of the 32 journals searched, 17 had no reference to information literacy throughout their life-spans, 5 had one reference, 3 had two references, 3 had four to six references and only 4 had more than six references. These searches were done over multiple years and covered multiple volumes of each journal.

To argue that over half of the best regarded journals in higher education today had never once made reference to information literacy may not tell the whole tale. There are, no doubt, many articles in these journals that deal with critical thinking and student research ability, terminology which at least contains elements of information literacy. Yet the reality remains that these findings demonstrate that there is very little crossover between the information literacy literature, developed to a sophisticated level by academic librarians, and higher education. While the term "information literacy" is sometimes criticized, even by its advocates, it is indeed *the* technical descriptor for this growing area of study and teaching. To have the term, therefore, appear in so few higher education journals says that the considerable information literacy literature found in books and journals within the library and information studies world is not being recognized by scholars in higher education.

Christine Bruce, commenting on information literacy discourse, writes:

> It has been evident that little of the literature is appearing in mainstream higher education journals or

discipline-based journals, suggesting that the transformation of the information literacy agenda from a library-centered issue to a mainstream educational issue is only beginning. (2001, p. 113)

Despite the years that have followed this article, her words still remain true today.

The perpetuated experience (osmosis) gap

Many faculty members have either forgotten their own process of information literacy development (Leckie, 1996, pp. 202–3) or remember it rather triumphantly, because they were always smarter and better at research than most of their fellow students. Either way, almost all faculty members learned whatever research abilities they possess by a process of trial and error and now have little memory of what it meant to be a neophyte student researcher.

Speaking from over 25 years of personal experience, and supported by multiple studies, this author would assert that a large number of graduate students, even of doctoral students, continue to struggle to pick up skills necessary for their thesis and dissertation research, the keener of them often depending heavily on librarians. To be even more brutally honest, many of these students have an uncanny ability to optimize highly inefficient research methods and somehow pull together a decent dissertation by sheer brilliance alone despite shabby skills. These students then take up professorial roles, never having learned how to navigate a journal database with skill, use controlled vocabularies to advantage, or even take on advanced features in a library catalog.

To get where they are, faculty members have often learned information research on their own, with minimal guidance. They somehow made it through, and learning to do research by doing research is the only training method they know. Is it, in fact, possible to teach people how to develop research abilities? It is indeed possible, but most faculty members have never actually seen it done and are not especially interested in attempting it themselves.

Leckie discussed the "expert researcher" model inhabited by faculty members. Professional academics work within narrow fields in which they have a strong understanding of their literature. For many of them, keeping up with a few journals and staying in contact with colleagues is more useful than doing the kinds of research performed by their students, who know little about the field they are studying and thus must cast a wider net to find relevant material for research projects. Leckie concludes, "The expert researcher simply cannot imagine (or refuses to think about) the continuum of problems that undergraduates have in using even a moderately-sized academic library" (ibid., p. 206).

Leckie and Fullerton (1999a) found that faculty members generally believe that students' research abilities improve over time. While professors have a weak understanding of how this occurs, they tend to think that students learn research skills on their own or consult librarians for instruction. The writers commented:

> Unfortunately, these views tend to perpetuate the type of individualistic trial-and-error learning environment that many faculty themselves experienced in graduate school but that does not develop the information literacy skills the majority of undergraduates today will need to be productive members of society. (ibid., pp. 14–15)

Bury (2011) has provided more recent corroboration that faculty at York University, Canada, believe students improve their research processes ability on their own over time. Though these faculty members saw some value in instruction, they were not giving priority to opportunities for such instruction.

Webber and Johnston's (2006) study of 80 professional academics in Britain found that most of them could not define "information literacy." Further, university faculty members believed that students really are picking up research skills, though these professors did not discuss such skills to any great extent with students and had little notion of what libraries were teaching.

McGuiness (2006) reported similar findings from a set of extensive faculty interviews. Professors generally believed that students absorb research skills by doing research and that advanced skill development comes out of student motivation and innate ability rather than instruction. Gaps in ability with research processes were blamed on the students. If they wanted such skills, they would get them. These same faculty members, however, were unable to articulate the process by which research skills were developed and had only a vague notion of the actual world of the average student doing research. McGuiness pointed out the resulting paradox. Students know they are unlikely to be graded directly on their research skills because faculty do not believe that student skills will improve to any great measure, so they do minimal work. But professors, thinking that research skills are to be learned by students on their own, fail to provide instruction or assignments intended to develop research ability.

Weetman (2005), in a study of academic faculty at De Montfort University, UK, found that over 90 percent believed that students, once they had completed their higher education programs, would have become information-literate to the level demanded by standards such as those of the Association of College and Research Libraries and SCONUL. Yet these faculty members could point to few activities in their classes intended either to teach or assess information and research skills, especially those related to acquiring information.

Information literacy by osmosis thus remains an untested belief, scarcely more than a hopeful assumption. Most research of student information literacy demonstrates that it does not happen or that gains in ability without training are minimal. Students, without significant instruction, do not learn to do research well simply by doing research.

Faulty assumptions about students and technology

Oblinger and Hawkins point out a reality that has long been observed by librarians: "Whereas colleges and universities often focus on technology skills, it is actually *information literacy* that should be the concern. Information literacy is much more than knowing how to open a Web browser and type a search term into Google" (2006, p. 12). It is quite amazing, in fact, to read the numerous studies, reports and educational plans built around "harnessing technology for education," and then to observe how few of these publications ever mention information literacy or even describe its components.

The myth that technological ability equals information and research ability seems to have convinced the best minds in educational thinking today (Jenson, 2004). As large numbers of studies have demonstrated, however, our highly technological students continue to fail miserably at most aspects of sophisticated information handling.

This problem, in fact, may be both deeper and more subtle than simply constituting a false mythology. The fact is that much technology used by *professors* in today's higher education environment is sporadic, and decidedly "old school" in a world in which Facebook and text messaging are the technological landmarks of our students and PowerPoint is a Dark Ages application. Academia's version of technology is often very much behind the times. Selwyn (2007) points out that the emphasis on making our students technologically literate with academic tools that they find anachronistic both limits their creative use of information technology and actually leads them to boycott or opt out of academic information technology entirely.

A study by Grant, Malloy and Murphy (2009) has demonstrated that student ability with even basic computing software, such as word processors and spreadsheets, is less sophisticated than we, or students themselves, believe. But, even if we were to grant that university students have a sound knowledge of the latest technology, this does not necessarily mean that they will be good researchers. Head, in a study of students at a small liberal arts college, concludes:

> These findings suggest that, even though young people may have been exposed to computers since they learned the alphabet and may be avid users of sites like MySpace and YouTube, college-aged students are no more likely to be natural-born researchers and scholars than anyone else. Conducting research remains a formidable task, one that must be learned through instruction and honed with practice – a fact that librarians have known for ages. (2008, p. 437)

The recent trend among professors, in their own research, to use Web tools like Google Scholar in preference to more complex but also more sophisticated library databases is not helping matters (Housewright and Schonfeld, 2008). There seems to be a general assumption among many academics that information is becoming more accessible and that search tools are easier to use. This may be true in one sense, in that a search engine like Google Scholar demands little knowledge of search techniques. But such tools produce very large result sets comprising a confusing number of types of academic literature. The illusion of ease and effectiveness thus becomes simply that – an illusion – when one considers that the end product is both mystifying and much less precise than resources found through a subscribed library database. Falsely assuming that Google Scholar is simple and sufficient may make academics less inclined to teach students how to use an EBSCO or Gale database.

Faculty culture

The information literacy movement and the major initiatives for teaching research processes in universities have come primarily from academic libraries and library organizations (though organizations like UNESCO have also been strong supporters). The idea of putting research processes education into the curriculum has not been supported at all strongly by teaching professors in the various disciplines.

Bennett, discussing the work of those who promote information literacy within academia wrote: "Their advocacy often encounters a campus environment that, although rarely hostile, is often uniformed, indifferent, or occupied with other priorities" (2007, p. 148). If information literacy is as important as its advocates assert, why then does it receive so little notice among teaching faculty? One answer may well be faculty culture.

Faculty members in theory are interested in improving their students' research abilities, but study after study demonstrates that they are not inclined to sacrifice classroom time to do so (Cannon, 1994; Leckie and Fullerton, 1999a; Hrycaj and Russo, 2007; Bury, 2011). As Webber and Johnston (2006), in a study of 80 academics, argued:

> Most are unwilling to give more than an hour of their class time to information literacy, and many will not even give that much ... Most academics would be unwilling to involve librarians in curriculum design e.g. feeling that it was a waste of time or inappropriate.

The value of Larry Hardesty's (1995) study of faculty culture to this issue can scarcely be overestimated. Hardesty demonstrated that at the heart of librarian-faculty mutual misunderstanding (and thus struggles with getting information literacy onto the academic agenda) is the interplay of two distinct cultures. Whereas librarians typify a "managerial culture" of goals, collegiality and a concern for the broader educational requirements of the student, faculty culture emphasizes "research, content and specialization," with a "de-emphasis on teaching, process and undergraduates." The supreme value among faculty members is professional autonomy, whose corollary is academic freedom. Professors, as well, according to Hardesty, typically face a chronic shortage of time to fulfill their tasks and are resistant to change. Librarians, seeking to meet broad student informational needs and help professors develop skills that go beyond the bounds of any particular subject discipline, are thus viewed by faculty members as intruders.

Baker pointed out what may well be a related complication of faculty culture – the fact that faculty within discipline-related focus groups studying goals for information literacy assignments tended not to see the issue in terms of broader skills for lifelong learning and the marketplace, but framed "the student library assignment decision around narrower and more directly impactive pedagogical and educational questions, such as familiarity with the literature in a specific discipline" (1997, p. 177). That is, faculty members think in terms of content, and specifically content within their own disciplines, rather than in terms of process and skill development that can be transferable to a wider range of subjects.

Leckie and Fullerton (1999b) used the language of pedagogical discourse to explain the distinctiveness of faculty and librarian perceptions of their roles. Their conclusion was:

> Faculty are participating in discourses that serve to protect their disciplines, preserve their own disciplinary expertise and academic freedom, and uphold self-motivated, individualistic learning. Librarians are employing the pedagogical discourses related to meeting user needs, teaching important generic skills and providing efficient service.

These researchers further pointed out that faculty pedagogy seeks to maintain control of the classroom, thus making it difficult for librarians to encroach into faculty-held territory.

Another element of faculty culture that helps ensure that research processes education does not achieve prominence in the curriculum comes from the way in which experts do research. The linear conceptions of thesis/question development, research in books, then in journals, and so on, that are part of information literacy instruction are relatively foreign to expert researchers. Stoan (1991) summarized a significant number of studies showing that expert researchers rely upon citation gleaning, reading of current journals, and interaction with colleagues for the majority of their research information. What is more, experts follow a distinctly non-linear path in doing informational research, drawing information and ideas from a wide variety of sources, all the while revising and rethinking until the project is completed. The notion of an informational research "method" is thus foreign to many professors, who would be unable to articulate one, since their research patterns change from project to project.

If faculty, indeed, do research in non-linear ways, it is not surprising that offers by librarians to help faculty members teach their students better research methods can tend to fall on deaf or resistant ears. Research among subject experts is not a linear process that can be taught. You simply get in there and shape a research project or literature review by whatever means you have available. There is no consistent method.

Students, on the other hand, lacking the knowledge content and discourse expertise of their professors, require exactly what their professors reject – a set of steps or strategies to make sense of their research problems, identify and acquire needed data in several formats, compile and evaluate the data and organize it into a final project. Without the support of a knowledge base and years of experience in working with it, students lack the basic skills and understanding needed to avoid floundering.

Kempcke (2002) argued that things may have changed since Hardesty. Many institutions are re-evaluating core curriculum, and the ACRL "Competency Standards for Higher Education" have put pressure on academia to take information literacy seriously. That might one day actually be the case, but there appears to be little evidence in the current higher educational literature of any movement toward a generalized embrace of information literacy by academics.

Is faculty culture an obstacle to ensuring that students become information-literate? Faculty would certainly deny any such accusation, arguing that their work of teaching the content and critical thinking skills inherent to their disciplines is information literacy at its best. Information literacy, however, as defined by those who have set standards for it, is anchored, not just in content with a little critical thinking thrown in, but in process. Librarians, who generally focus more on process, find themselves hard-pressed to convince faculty that knowledge of content (and even ability to think critically within content) is insufficient to make most people truly information-literate (Badke, 2005).

This is supported by Sterngold (2008), himself a faculty member who has worked cooperatively with an academic librarian to deliver research processes instruction in marketing courses. Sterngold argues that librarians should tone down their rhetoric about information literacy, simplify their definitions to terms that faculty can understand, and give up their teaching role in favor of serving as consultants to faculty, who would do the information literacy instruction. At the same time, he admits that, "Many faculty members remain apathetic and uniformed about IL" (ibid., p. 86). As well, "Most faculty members are preoccupied with covering as much subject matter as possible in their courses, and they are not interested in devoting any more time to developing students' information competencies" (ibid., p. 87). One wonders, then, how faculty would ever be motivated to teach information literacy themselves, as Sterngold prefers. A similar lack of priority given by faculty to teaching research processes was found in Bury's (2011) study at York University, Canada.

Faculty perception of librarians

Faculty members do not generally see librarians as full academic colleagues and thus have little appreciation for librarians as instructors (Saunders, 2009). This perception arises from the fact that librarians often have terminal Master's degrees, have limited teaching experience, and tend not to publish as much as do classroom faculty (McGuinness, 2006, p. 575).

Many professors have not understood, however, the extent to which technology has changed both student culture and the information environment, territories which are common ground to librarians. Perhaps, out of a failure to put themselves and their skills forward, librarians, in turn, have not been able to demonstrate their amazing knowledge of and ability with information literacy pedagogy in a highly technologized setting. This is less a content-oriented competency (though there is content, to be sure) than a facility with handling information in its new environment and passing that facility along to students. Not having been given the chance to do much more than one-shot instruction sessions, many librarians have yet to demonstrate what they could offer if research processes instruction were given its due within the curriculum.

The hesitation of accrediting bodies

The following discussion relates more to the American situation where higher education institutions are accredited using accrediting agencies sanctioned by the federal government, than it may to other countries that have other ways of determining educational quality. For other countries, what follows, however, is still instructive in that it shows how seldom those who set the educational standards for our institutions actually take research processes instruction seriously.

Of the six major accrediting bodies for higher education in the United States, only one – the Middle States Commission on Higher Education – has given significant emphasis to information literacy. All of the others mention it only briefly if, indeed, they use the term "information literacy" at all in their standards statements.

We might wonder why this is the case, if information literacy has indeed been endorsed by the significant library associations and any number of higher education associations that are well accepted within academia. Accrediting bodies do, after all, have the authority to compel the meeting of standards, do they not?

The fact is that accreditation is something more of a dance than an exercise of dictatorship. Accrediting bodies, while monopolies for their constituencies, know that keeping a distinction between what is doable and what may not be is in their best interests. These bodies, in turn, are responsible to the U.S. Department of Education's Office of Postsecondary Education for their own recognition as viable agencies, so that draconian requirements may well put them in jeopardy.

Still, the Middle States Commission has been able to produce extremely valuable resources and guidelines for its institutions without creating a riot of discontent (Middle States Commission on Higher Education, 2003, 2009), so the hesitation of the other agencies to advance the information literacy cause may well lie in areas other than fear of displeasing their constituencies.

Conclusion

We have looked at several reasons why the teaching of research processes remains a low priority in academic life. These may be summarized with one potentially dangerous all-encompassing statement: *The teaching of research processes is not a priority because so few people recognize that there is a problem to address or a solution possible.* It is the nature of higher education (as undoubtedly most education) to perpetuate its past successes, even when the world changes, and to fail to recognize looming threats to its future.

The rise of information technology has created a new informational order as dramatically different from the old one as was the era of hand-copied manuscripts from that of the printing press. When the need for skills to link the right information to the right situation becomes as recognized as it should be, we can only hope that academia will awaken to that need and take up the means to help students navigate the new information age.

Note

This chapter is adapted from (Badke, 2011c). "Why information literacy is invisible". *Communications in Information Literacy*, Vol. 4, No. 2, pp. 129–41. Retrieved from: *http://thebrowers.net/comminfolit/index. php?journal=cil&page=article&op=viewFile&path[]=Vol4-2010PER3&path[]=119*

4

Current initiatives in research processes

Abstract: The early visions of an information-literate society have been followed by a number of sets of standards, which state goals and present criteria for measuring outcomes. Yet the primary means for research processes instruction in the academic world remains the single session which focuses more on library instruction than research ability and which falsely assumes that the ability gap in our students requires only a remedial remedy. Other methods, though more rare, include credit courses and programs of instruction through the curriculum. Ultimately, all such methods are inadequate – the one-shot because remedial instruction is not enough, the credit course because it is rare and offers only one opportunity for instruction, and through-the-curriculum because it is so difficult to sustain. The main difficulty with all current approaches is that they are not robust enough to meet the research processes ability needs of our students.

Key words: credit instruction, one-shots, remedial instruction, through-the-curriculum instruction.

Paul G. Zurkowski, who coined the term "Information Literacy," wrote this:

Information is not knowledge; it is concepts or ideas which enter a person's field of perception, are evaluated and assimilated, reinforcing or changing the individual's concept of reality and/or ability to act. As beauty is in the eye of the beholder, so information is in the mind of the user. (Zurkowski and National Commission on Libraries and Information Science, 1974, p. 1)

With these words, he opened the door to a new way of understanding our emerging information age. The simple concept of studying information itself as subject matter has turned into the information literacy movement of today.

Zurkowski's voice was prophetic. Even in 1974, he wrote that people were taking on an increasing variety of information-seeking procedures, resulting in a "multiplicity of access routes and sources" that had arisen to fulfill information needs. Yet, these new routes to information were "poorly understood and vastly underutilized." He set an agenda for the future by writing: "More and more of the events and artifacts of human existence are being dealt with in information equivalents, requiring retraining of the whole population" (ibid., p. 1).

To make his concept of information clear, Zurkowski wrote:

People trained in the application of information resources to their work can be called information literates. They have learned techniques and skills for utilizing the wide range of research tools as well as primary sources in molding information solutions to their problems. The individuals in the remaining portion of the population, while literate in the sense that they can read and write, do not have a measure for the value of information, do not have an ability to mold information to their needs, and realistically must be called information illiterates. (ibid., p. 6)

From the outset, several concepts were clear in Zurkowski's work. First, information is not knowledge until it is manipulated or "molded," as he expressed it. Second, knowing how to handle information so that it can be used effectively to solve problems is the essence of information literacy. Thus information can never be an end in itself but has to be enlisted as a tool to accomplish a purpose.

Bravely, Zurkowski estimated that perhaps one-sixth of the US population comprised information literates. The rest were in the "illiterates" category. Ongoing research since his time has made his estimate plausible, and it continues to be an intelligent guess. Zurkowski himself called for "a major national program to achieve universal information literacy by 1984" (ibid., p. 27), a program that sadly was never implemented by educators and government.

It is easy merely to dismiss the Paul Zurkowskis of this world as visionaries, ahead of their time. Zurkowski, to be sure, was not always able to foresee certain elements of the murky future (though he uncannily predicted the need for a national system for sharing information resources that would achieve the comprehensiveness of libraries without stealing the profits of publishers, and a "pluralism of channels of communication," thus foreshadowing the World Wide Web). Still, Zurkowski's vision of the information age has proven largely true – we are inundated by knowledge that needs to be harnessed to achieve goals, yet the skills of most of us, as we have seen, are limited.

Paul Zurkowski is not a librarian but was president of the Information Industry Association, which worked with companies producing information products. His vision of information literacy, however, was taken up primarily by academic librarians. Here the concept faced a challenge it is still trying to overcome – its association with the much older discipline of bibliographic instruction (library instruction).

Libraries, for more than a century, have been doing bibliographic instruction, essentially orienting their patrons to the proper use of tools and procedures for research within libraries. As such, the training has tended to be rather architectural – "Here is the book catalog and this is how to use it, here are the library stacks and notice the call numbers on the books," etc. To this day, "library instruction" as bibliographic instruction now calls itself, is a mainstay in many academic institutions.

Zurkowski's vision was much larger. He argued that not all information would be found in libraries but that national "data bases" would be formed to satisfy information needs that libraries could not provide. Zurkowski's goal was never simply to have a population that could use libraries well. It was to teach people, more or less universally, how to handle information in such a way that what they needed to know could easily be found and then put to profitable use. This larger vision encompasses what we are calling "research processes."

So, even as we look at the many facets of the information literacy movement that do capture Zukowski's vision, we need to recognize that there are vestiges of the older notion – that the way to teach people how to handle information is to teach them how to use a library. While using a library well may be one aspect of becoming information-literate, it is not nearly the whole story.

Development of standards among academic librarians

The rise of information literacy standards since the late 1990s helped the fledgling movement to define itself clearly, both for what it is and for what it is not. Standards have, as well, enabled information professionals to set benchmarks for teaching and assessment of specific information literacy skills. At the same time, any standards statement is a bit like a list of skills needed to drive a car ("Brake steadily with no jerking; steer directly with no drift, and so on"). It is only when considered together that the individual skills actually take on any real life. That said, standards can be very helpful.

The Association of College and Research Libraries "Information Literacy Competency Standards for Higher Education" (ACRL, 2000) are the best known of many sets of standards around the world. Officially sanctioned by ACRL, they are also endorsed by the American Association for Higher Education and the Council of Independent Colleges.

These standards are based on the information literacy definition promulgated by the American Library Association (ACLR, 1989): "To be information literate, a person must be able to recognize when information is needed and have the ability to locate, evaluate, and use effectively the needed information." According to the Association of College & Research Libraries, there are five major measures within the standards themselves:

The information-literate student determines the nature and extent of the information needed.

The information-literate student accesses needed information effectively and efficiently.

The information-literate student evaluates information and its sources critically and incorporates selected information into his or her knowledge base and value system.

The information-literate student, individually or as a member of a group, uses information effectively to accomplish a specific purpose.

The information-literate student understands many of the economic, legal, and social issues surrounding the use of information and accesses and uses information ethically and legally. (ACLR, 2000)

Each of the standards has its own sets of performance indicators and outcomes, thus giving it a basis for establishing assessment measures and developing rubrics. There is sufficient rigor in the standards to enable educators to determine whether or not a student has achieved the level of information literacy required.

To that set of standards have been added numerous accompanying standards documents, some related to specific subject disciplines (see the list at: http://www.ala.org/ala/mgrps/divs/acrl/about/sections/is/webarchive/infolitdisciplines/ildhome.cfm). The Association of American Colleges and Universities (2009) has provided rubrics for any standards that are similar to those of ACRL.

To meet a distinctive vision, the Australian and New Zealand Information Literacy Framework document (Bundy, 2004) adopted the ACRL standards with modifications, notably changing "the information literate student" to "the information literate person" and making a couple of modifications to the standards themselves. Its lineup is:

Standard One: The information-literate person recognises the need for information and determines the nature and extent of the information needed.

Standard Two: The information-literate person finds needed information effectively and efficiently.

Standard Three: The information-literate person critically evaluates information and the information seeking process.

Standard Four: The information-literate person manages information collected or generated.

Standard Five: The information-literate person applies prior and new information to construct new concepts or create new understandings.

Standard Six: The information-literate person uses information with understanding and acknowledges cultural, ethical, economic, legal, and social issues surrounding the use of information.

In 1999, at roughly the same time that the ACRL standards were being developed, the Society of College, National & University Libraries (SCONUL) in Britain, developed what it referred to as the "Seven Headline Skills" or "Seven Pillars" of information literacy. These have since been updated as the SCONUL Seven Pillars of Information Literacy: Core Model for Higher Education, and include the following:

IDENTIFY – Able to identify a personal need for information.

SCOPE – Can assess current knowledge and identify gaps.

PLAN – Can construct strategies for locating information and data.

GATHER – Can locate and access the information and data they need.

EVALUATE – Can review the research process and compare and evaluate information and data.

MANAGE – Can organise information professionally and ethically.

PRESENT – Can apply the knowledge gained: presenting the results of their research, synthesising new and old information and data to create new knowledge and disseminating it in a variety of ways. (SCONUL Working Group on Information Literacy, 2011)

While not as popular worldwide as the ACRL statement, the SCONUL standards have the advantage of more directly following a narrative of actual research processes than does ACRL. As with all such standards, SCONUL does not focus particularly on libraries but upon the stages required for effective informational research. The standards include measures both of understanding and of ability, thus providing a rubric to determine if a student is able to accomplish the research processes desired in higher education.

There are numerous sets of national and regional standards, as well as an increasing number of standards related to pre-university. Together, they encapsulate a good representation of the requirements and measures of research ability, at least in a generic sense. What most of them lack is a disciplinary emphasis, though ACRL has gathered links to various discipline-related standards, many of them are incomplete (ACRL, 2011).

Meanwhile, information literacy has taken on international importance, from President Obama's declaration of National Information Literacy Awareness Month in October 2009 (Obama, 2009), to international declarations of information literacy goals and principles in Prague and Alexandria (The Prague Declaration, 2003; Garner, 2006). Sturges and Gastinger (2010), based on intimations in several national and international initiatives, have argued that information literacy should be considered a human right. Yet the reality of limited actual instruction in research processes (information literacy) belies the hyperbole found in many position statements.

Remedial instruction

The most common method for providing training in research processes is a single class taught either as a generic orientation or as a subject-specific session, the latter often in conjunction with a student assignment. Most such sessions are library or database orientations only and are generally taught by librarians at the invitation of subject professors. For larger universities, the sheer number of students who must be reached generally precludes much more than one such training venture per student per degree program. The librarians who teach these sessions tend to feel both rushed and stressed, often considering the results in actual student learning to be minimal.

An alternative approach is "point of need" instruction in which students drop into voluntary sessions designed to achieve specific research learning goals. On a more one-to-one basis, librarian reference interviews with students can serve a "point of need" purpose, though the amount of instruction provided depends both on student tolerance of it and amount of time available to the reference librarian.

Technology has provided options for alternate delivery of the content of one-shots. One of these is the short animated tutorial, for which a leading vehicle is the collaborative Animated Tutorials Sharing Project (A.N.T.S., 2011), of which this author is a founding member. See my institution's own complex of locally created tutorials at *http://www.twu.ca/library/flashtutorials.htm* (most of these courtesy of my talented colleague, Duncan Dixon). Another technological approach is a quiz-based tutorial program within university courseware that allows students to do actual searches in academic databases in order to answer specific questions based on the results of their work (Badke, 2009b).

The single (or "one-shot") session, along with online tutorials, has become the industry norm for information literacy despite their inadequacies, primarily because finance, logistics, and academic priorities in many institutions dictate this to be the default approach. Yet the deficiencies of the short-term option are quite apparent.

First, it assumes that learning research processes is a remedial task, that is, something that requires only minimal training. The presumption here is that the student has something of a deficit, but a session or two will fix it. This, as we have already seen, is not the case when such a presumption is put to the test. Learning research processes is a complex task more like learning a new language than learning how to tie your shoelaces. Unfortunately, the very fact that the single session is so predominant creates circular thinking: For logistical and historical reasons, most students get about an hour or so of information literacy instruction during the course of their degrees. Since students are able to graduate with only one-shots behind them, the one-shots must be doing the job, and information literacy must, therefore, be an easily resolved remedial problem.

Second, the one-shot remedial approach assumes that the primary learning challenge is that students do not know how to use the library and/or use databases well. Thus the teaching of research processes tends to get focused down to teaching how to do searches for resources. Like learning how to add an app to a mobile device, learning how to use library tools seems like a simple task. Show them how, give them a test, and they are set. But such thinking fails to take into account the reality that searching using library tools is part of a much larger complex of research processes understandings and skills. Such a process begins with defining a question and ends with assessing and using the resources found to address the problem. Nor does a remedial approach include the reality that, before the research process begins, the student must have a grasp of the nature of the resources that define the literature available.

Third, the one-shot, even when it is done in the context of a subject discipline, does not provide the student with the particular nuances of the research process done within that discipline. To have insider information regarding what is demanded by practitioners of the discipline, what types of information are crucial, how cases and alternatives are argued in the discipline, what constitutes good evidence, and so on, are essential to good research. None of that is remedial but is at the core of education. It cannot be taught within a single session.

The one-shot can be a useful introduction, but it should never be seen as even remotely sufficient to develop significant student understanding and skills in research processes.

Credit-based courses

The seeming Holy Grail of research processes instruction has been the "for credit" course, if, of course, anyone can convince academic administrators to institute one, let alone make it required. The intention of a credit information literacy course is to cover the whole research process from topic selection to the point at which the final research project is written. As such, the intention is laudable in that it overcomes the sense that teaching research processes is a remedial task.

Such courses, however, are rare in comparison with the "one-shot." When offered as electives, they tend to be poorly attended, because, as we have seen, most students overestimate their research ability and thus do not see such a course as necessary. Truth to tell, those same students generally view such a course offering as potentially uninteresting and probably more difficult than it needs to be.

Compulsory credit courses within university disciplines or as graduation requirements are even rarer. The Primary Research Group (2008), in a study of American and Canadian academic institutions, found that less than 6 percent of them offered required credit information literacy courses. Where they are found, they tend to persist and to achieve their goals, and the fact that they are required appears to be the key to their success.

The problem of needing to respond to disciplinary variability in teaching research processes is compounded by the fact that, for credit information, literacy courses are generally taught by librarians rather than by subject-specific professors. Thus they tend to take on more of a generic flavor, de-emphasizing the nuances of the disciplines. While there are certainly some commonalities in the research processes of various disciplines – problem identification, use of databases, evaluation of resources, and so on – there are also discipline-specific abilities – problem statement formulation, types of databases used in specific subject areas, types of evidence valued and for what reasons, etc.

My essay on the topic (Badke, 2003) somewhat optimistically argued that it was time to get the teaching of research out of the library and into the academy. The academy, in turn, needed to be convinced that a discipline-specific course lodged in each subject major would meet the higher goals of the discipline by training students to understand and use information critically, thus becoming skilled researchers.

The challenge, however, is to justify the creation of a new research processes course, a course that is required as part of the core offerings of the discipline. What is more, such a course would have to be taught within each discipline. For those involved in curriculum creation, the nature of the problem is obvious – curricula do not generally have room for new offerings unless some existing course is removed. To justify a course in research processes as more important than an existing course is a daunting prospect, which is why curricula so seldom change. While I may genuinely believe that research processes courses in history, English literature, sociology and chemistry would revolutionize student ability to partake in disciplinary thinking, I would have to be exceedingly convincing to make the case for dropping an existing course previously deemed essential.

What is more, librarians, who understand the teaching of research processes well, would need to collaborate with subject specialist professors after convincing those professors of the importance of these new courses. It can be done (for example, University of Alberta. Augustana, 2007, 2011), but the statistics show that such courses, especially as full sets of discipline-specific offerings within institutions, are rare.

An emerging, hopeful trend is the development of research and writing courses. The Primary Research Group (2008) study found that up to 25 percent of universities had at least one research and writing course offering. Such courses can, indeed, form a means for discipline-specific professors to work with librarians. There is a tendency, however, for the "research" portion of the course to get rather short shrift in contrast to the writing portion. With limited teaching time for research processes, students may not acquire sufficient understanding and ability to learn to do research with any real sophistication. Still, this is a potentially useful option (see Badke, 2011a, for an example).

Credit-bearing research courses do work when they are given an opportunity. My own twenty plus years of experience with a graduate research course in our seminary division has provided ample evidence that it is possible to teach discipline-specific research processes within a required credit course (Badke, 2010b).

Instruction through the curriculum

Another option is through-the-curriculum research processes instruction. This approach is much closer to our current quest for an optimum model in that it addresses the need for disciplinary emphasis and provides a venue for ongoing skill development. While the single course model just discussed provides only a single in-depth opportunity to learn research processes, the tenets of good pedagogy would argue that complex abilities need to be learned over time in a variety of settings and involve a considerable amount of practical experience. The through-the-curriculum approach answers that need.

If we provide numerous opportunities within a student's program to learn components of, and improve upon, research processes, we have what appears to be an ideal educational situation. The key to the success of any through-the curriculum venture, however, is careful planning and coordination. There must be significant agreement among academic administrators and faculty members that such an initiative is needed, as well as very careful organization of the ways and means by which it can be carried out. Program goals must be studied and courses identified both to determine venues for each aspect of training and to identify the training purposes to be achieved in each designated course. Professors need to be able and willing to provide the needed educational experience or else specialists need to be brought in.

Therein lies the rub for through-the-curriculum plans to teach research processes. They require a tremendous amount of "buy in" from all concerned, along with the infrastructure to ensure that they succeed in all of their disparate elements. This is particularly true if the initiative comes from administrators rather than from instructors at the grassroots level. Typically, such campus-wide efforts begin with enthusiasm, then founder, unless they are sustained in significant and deliberate ways.

There are numerous examples of successful and also less than successful implementation in the literature. Brown and Nelson (2003), for example, describe a through-the-curriculum program within a medical school. Key to its success was a careful plan, instruction primarily by librarians and some training for faculty members. Also highly relevant was the fact that the medical school curriculum stressed "Informatics," that is, the acquisition and use of relevant data in order to make informed decisions regarding medical practice. This concept is closely akin to that of "Evidence-Based Medicine." Thus there was a significant motivation for both faculty and students to be engaged in developing skilled research processes throughout the institution. See also Bent and Stockdale (2009).

One of the best manuals for implementation of through-the-curriculum programs of research processes development is that of the Middle States Commission on Higher Education (2003). Its core concept is as follows:

> Information literacy supports pedagogy focused on the development of effective research, critical thinking, and writing or other communication skills. Most faculty can identify these key characteristics in courses they currently are teaching. Instead of creating new courses based on an entirely new concept, the current classes faculty teach can become starting points for creating a more structured information literacy initiative, one in which information literacy strategies are incorporated within courses in the major fields of study. (ibid., p. 5)

The Middle States manual suggests a combination of stand-alone courses and instruction within courses in the curriculum. As a vision, this approach is exemplary and congruent with the suggestions ultimately to be made in this book. Where it is liable to fail is in the sheer amount of motivation and organizational structure needed to sustain it. Administrators have to devote resources to ensure that learning goals are met at the various instruction points designated. Faculty members need both the will and the expertise to carry out the instruction effectively, factors which are not to be assumed, given our earlier conclusion that academia as a whole does not tend to see the information literacy problem as significant.

The essential failure of all such initiatives

The amount of activity devoted to studying and trying to implement research processes education should be encouraging to most devotees of information literacy, but the reality is that much of the literature being produced by the growing information literacy movement is found within the circles of librarians and information professionals, not in the mainstream academic community. While there are scattered instances of universities and even nations or geographical regions adopting information literacy educational criteria and using them to develop programs with measurable outcomes, there are few institutional, let alone national, strategies that are actually succeeding at the level of comprehensive instruction. With all the energy being put into agendas for information literacy, we should surely by now be seeing significant results in student populations. But studies continue to report that most students are not exhibiting research processes knowledge and skills that meet the common standards, such as those of ACRL or SCONUL.

Part of the difficulty is that many initiatives tend to see the teaching of research processes as imparting a series of basic skill sets, with the implication that corresponding training opportunities will make students literate with information. This is overly optimistic when one considers the knowledge base that accompanies true information literacy: What is information (or can we even speak of "information" as a singular entity in our postmodern age)? Where does it come from? Who determines that it is published or that it takes the form that it does? What is the difference between a scholarly journal article and a webpage (or is that even a legitimate question, considering the confluence of formats available for information today)? Why do we have to pay for some information while we do not have to pay for other information? What is metadata, and how can it help us? What are the implications of electronic searching and electronic documents for the way we do research? How do we evaluate what we have found? What are the legal and ethical considerations that will have an impact on what is available to us and what is usable in our context?

It is one thing to create a tutorial or hold a class to teach someone how to search a database. It is quite another to help that same person in depth and/or over time to navigate the troubled waters of the information revolution with such skill that research problems are stated clearly and the right information for the task is effectively and efficiently found, evaluated, and used to optimum advantage within legal and ethical boundaries. Teachers of research processes all too often concentrate on skill sets (Corrall, 2007) while the overarching framework of understanding the nature and proper use of various information sources (the philosophy of information) is simply not taught, though it is clearly delineated in standards like those of ACRL (2000).

Another challenge to teaching research processes in depth comes from the ever-present reality that subject faculty still tend to see information literacy instructors as intruders and thus remain resistant to implementing the instruction they represent, beyond allowing them into the occasional class session for "library instruction." Information literacy is not generally on the agenda, in any significant way, of the average history or sociology or physics class, even though its students are expected to use the skills of information literacy in course assignments (Hardesty, 1995; Badke, 2005; Bury 2011).

A great deal of what passes for information literacy is still old-style bibliographic instruction in the form of single sessions that major on library use. There are, to be sure, strategic initiatives in university systems such as those of California State University (2007) and The Five Colleges of Ohio (2003), as well as national initiatives like the Big Blue of Britain (The Big Blue) and the Australian and New Zealand Information Literacy Framework (Bundy, 2004). But most universities and university systems lack such comprehensive programs. The statement by Johnston and Webber (2003) that UK universities are characterized by "a limited appreciation of the wider implications of the information society for higher education curricula, teaching and learning," summarizes the findings of many studies worldwide.

As a result of tentative and abortive efforts to make the teaching of research processes a viable part of higher education, the movement, even as it is growing, is beginning to run out of energy. In 2005, the Canadian Library Association conference included an agenda item entitled, "The Great Debate: Be it Resolved that we Teach them Nothing – Library Instruction Doesn't Work" (Canadian Library Association, 2005). To be sure, the proponent view failed, and the conference's business meeting passed a resolution to make information literacy a priority in its advocacy, but the fact that this was even debated at national level shows cause for concern.

The 2006 ACRL President's Program at the American Theological Library Association convention of June 2006 was a debate on the resolution: "The Emperor Has No Clothes: Be It Resolved That Information Literacy Is a Fad and Waste of Librarians' Time and Talent" (Downes, 2006). Such a debate in no way proves that information literacy is dead, but it does signal a growing opposition based primarily on the premise that what has been promised in this movement has not been delivered in terms of real advances within universities.

Why, then, given the power of so many initiatives in its favor, is information literacy struggling to find a place in higher education? Librarians might blame subject faculty and academic administrators who refuse to advance the information literacy agenda. Librarians may further feel that those in academia see little need to increase the role of information literacy in the curriculum and rarely understand what the information literacy movement is seeking to accomplish. Front line information literacy instructors could point to the enormous number of single sessions that they teach to a bored and resentful student body. The academy in general could argue that the segregation of information literacy research within publications that only librarians read tends to make the whole movement peripheral.

The following chapters will argue that, while all of these factors may be part of the problem, the real failure of information literacy to this point is that it is *simply not robust enough*. To invoke the metaphor expressed by Peter Drucker (Harris, 1993), our students should be playing Beethoven with research processes, but instead we get "Mary Had a Little Lamb." To this challenge we now turn.

5

The role of disciplinary thinking in research processes

Abstract: A paradigm shift is needed to make the teaching of research processes what it needs to be. Central to such a shift will be an invitation to students to enter into our disciplines. Each discipline, as a combination of philosophy (epistemology), method and application, embodies one or more metanarratives, that is, explanations of why we do what we do. While experts understand their metanarratives well, students do not. In fact, lack of subject and research process expertise may well be a significant reason why students stay outside our disciplines, learning about but not actually participating in them. Students require a consistent model for the research processes they are learning (we suggest the scientific model). More than that, they require that their professors find a radically new way to invite them into the disciplines they are studying.

Key words: application, epistemology, metanarratives, method, paradigm shift, scientific model.

We have come to an impasse. Information literacy is, indeed, the largest blind spot in higher education today, but the chances of ever making it what it needs to be seem remote. We must consider a paradigm shift that goes beyond merely opening the curriculum to some library instruction sessions, or having a librarian help develop some research exercises. The gap in research processes ability is an endemic issue, infecting everything we do in education. Why? Because information handling is at the foundation of any form of study you can imagine.

The barriers to developing skilled student researchers seem almost insurmountable – lack of understanding of the problem within academia, lack of space in the curriculum, lack of administrative support for information literacy initiatives, lack of desire among many faculty to make significant changes to tried and true patterns of education, and a pervasive argument that teaching research processes is someone else's task, if they can be taught at all.

That is why the bulk of all information literacy instruction today is done by librarians within short sessions, generally one hour or less. In many institutions, this amounts to nothing more than a single session throughout a student's entire undergraduate program. Considering the glaring need for information-literate graduates, it seems inconceivable that the teaching of research processes is so marginalized, but that is what we have. For every rare extensive program, there are dozens of institutions that have paid only lip service to the problem.

Webber and Johnston, commenting on short-term information literacy, wrote:

> The result may be a learning and teaching strategy which fails to engage the student at anything but the most superficial level. The student may gain a few tactics which enable him or her to negotiate some specific information sources. However, the student does not become information literate, capable of engaging in a fast-changing information society. (2000, p. 385)

The result for the marketplace is that workers, who depend on information for much of what they do, have a poor understanding of the nature of the information they are working with, waste huge amounts of time acquiring it (if they find it at all), and use it in inappropriate ways that put the enterprises they work for at risk (Kirton and Barham, 2005). When we consider all that information literacy entails, a much more comprehensive solution is required.

The development of scholarly ability within a discipline – content and process

Information literacy, the ability to handle information with skill and understanding within research processes, is not a matter for remedial instruction. The task of teaching research processes is akin to learning a new language. It requires long-term development that is progressive and constant over a significant period of time. We will argue shortly that students will only become information literate when information literacy becomes part of the foundation of their education.

How that is best accomplished has a great deal to do with having students begin to *do* higher educational disciplines, rather than acquiring just what constitutes a discipline's knowledge base. Essentially, educators are going to need to move from teaching *about* their disciplines to enabling their students to become disciplinarians. The expression, "Welcome to my world," encapsulates the goal. We need to educate, not merely to inform. We must invite students into our world and there reproduce ourselves in them, turning our students into active practitioners in our disciplines.

At the heart of such an endeavor is the task of understanding for ourselves how our disciplines work, how they have formed themselves, not just as bodies of knowledge but as entities akin to living beings with both content and processes that allow them to "live." Fear not, however. This is not as esoteric as it may appear.

What do we mean when we use the term "discipline?" In most regards the whole idea of a discipline is an artificial construction. Disciplines arose out of necessity: Historically, as knowledge expanded with the rise of the printing press, it became impossible for any one scholar to have expertise in everything. Thus academia began defining areas of knowledge that had discrete boundaries and a critical mass of published research and researchers built around them. It was not that each discipline lived in its own isolated universe bearing no relationship to any other discipline, but that, internally, there was enough going on within the discipline that it gained its own recognition and ongoing viability within the broader academic enterprise.

Essentially, then, what makes a discipline a discipline is a sufficient number of publications and practitioners within strict bounds of subject matter, as well as a perceived legitimacy of the discipline by academics in general. This latter element is crucial. Merely producing a lot of research or academic discourse within an area of study does not legitimate a discipline, as is clear from ongoing controversies over such proposed disciplines as parapsychology. Rather, the legitimacy of any discipline is determined by its recognition within the academic community.

Essential to a discipline are three factors: Philosophy, method, and application. Let us consider each in turn with regard to the way in which it addresses the information and research processes it encompasses.

Philosophy: epistemology of information

"Epistemology" is a philosophical concept that considers the nature of the sources of information we value. It asks questions like these: *Where does our disciplinary information come from? What forms does it take? Why is such information seen as significant to our discipline? How do we determine what sources are reliable/valuable and what are not?* For those of us who have functioned for some time within a particular discipline, our epistemology is second nature. Not only do we not think much about why we value some forms of information over others, but we might be hard-pressed to teach our epistemology to others. Still, knowing where our information comes from and what significance it has for the work we do is vital to the foundation of disciplinary work. It is also a realm neither understood nor properly appreciated by our students. If their ability with research processes is going to grow, they are going to have to understand the nature of the information field within which they are working.

Helping us are all those "philosophy of" or "theory of" introductory courses that students dread and many faculty members dislike teaching. Why do we teach them? Often because they are seen as essential to knowing a subject area, though it is not at all clear what is essential about them. If we were to think in terms of epistemology, however – how we know what we know, what are our information sources, and why we value some more than others – we might be able to justify the importance of "philosophy of" courses that teach just those elements.

For now, let's delve a bit deeper into epistemology. A sudden descent like this into philosophical thinking may seem challenging to the attention span, but it is important.

There was a time in which the concept of "information" could be summed up as "that which gives us the foundation for discovering truth." Postmodernism and Poststructuralism have challenged the assumption that the sources of our information are objective and values-neutral enough to make the acquiring and use of information a sure path to truth. Kapitzke (2003), for example, has argued that information can no longer be seen as operating in some sort of vacuum, separated from the social and historical processes that shape it and justify its existence. Information is not neutral, nor is it apolitical.

Kapitzke goes on to call for us to recognize a hyperliteracy (a literacy that recognizes the various forms and media in which information is found) as a better explanation of the many environmental factors operating when information is created and used. Hyperliteracy includes "intermediality," the idea that we must view the information process within the worlds of both its producer and user. The one who created the information may not live within the conceptual environment of the one who uses the information, creating a situation in which there is a disconnection between the intent of the creator and the interpretation of the user. Recognizing this reality will help us maintain a constant analysis of the cultures and assumptions of both creator and user.

This idea, that information always is contextual and exists in tension between producers and users, is helpful, yet it neglects one aspect of epistemology – the reality that a source of information needs to be evaluated by criteria that are more or less universally acceptable. We may contextualize the information process, but we must agree upon the interpretive means we employ to recognize what the writer writes, how the information became published, and how the reader reads it. Also, a proper epistemology looks at the qualifications, presuppositions and biases of the writer as well as of the reader.

Here our students need to learn how to use commonly accepted criteria that help them judge the extent to which they can believe, rely upon, or use the information according to the purpose it for which it was created. Unless our epistemology makes a god of subjectivity, any philosophy of knowledge has to ask questions like, "Who wrote this? Does she have the required knowledge base to make her writing reliable? What presuppositions have set the direction for her approach to this topic? What biases do I bring to my reading of her work? What value will this piece of information ultimately have to my quest?"

Academic information generally lives within the context of a subject discipline. In a subject discipline, discourse is carried out by specific though often unwritten rules that make any particular piece of evidence or product of research either valid or invalid, based on the criteria established by the discipline. We might well accept the famous warning of Martin (1998) regarding political bias within disciplines, but Keresztesi (1982) has made it clear in his pioneering article, "The Science of Bibliography," that the recognition of an area of study as a discipline within the university is the only way for it to achieve widespread approval in society.

This tells us that, though bias may exist within the creator, the publisher, and the reader, we still need ground rules that will guide us in our recognition of the value of information sources and in the means we use to understand them. Epistemological issues are not insignificant ones. Students who understand the forces at work in the production and validation of information sources in their disciplines are prepared to use information intelligently, effectively and ethically to address the research needs which they are facing.

The methodology of the information quest: finding a research model

The teaching of research processes in disciplines, when it is done at all, is seldom built around a coherent research methodology. Part of the problem has been the fact that much of what we have done in the past to attempt the teaching of research processes has really been bibliographic instruction that focuses on the library and its search tools, thus missing the concept that research involves larger processes. Even when we have a clear epistemology in place, the idea of a guiding *methodology* that shows students how to move from points A to B to C is often lost in the rush to move our instruction from philosophy to application. Thus, while we may teach about the sources of our information, we skip research method in favor of showing students how to use search tools. This creates a library-based architectural model of instruction – here is the catalog, these are the databases, and here is how you use them. Students are left with a box of tools but no blueprint for the project.

We require some way to guide students from the beginning to the end in their research, encompassing all aspects of it. This works best if we employ and teach a research model that enables students to have a clear mental picture of the research task. Commonly, students spin their wheels at the beginning of any piece of research, trying to understand the topic they are working on and struggling to find a direction to take both in finding the information needed and in determining what to do with it in order to produce a coherent product (Head and Eisenberg, 2010). They rarely have a concept of the process involved in moving from start to end. This is what a research model could provide. It would, in essence, explain both the nature of research and the steps required to pursue it.

Research models, however, are open to criticism. The widely used information processing paradigm (McGuire, 1972) that sees a progression from data to information to knowledge has been criticized by many as being too structured and not open enough to the possibility that information can just as easily lead to confusion.

Marcum (2002), in particular, has pointed out that knowledge is not organized information but a quantum leap from information to cognition, understanding and experience. He argues: "Knowledge is not certainty but is a set of beliefs about causal relationships between phenomena" (ibid., p. 12).

Marcum further points out that the information processing model, as well as most information literacy models, fails to take into account the crucial role of the researcher in formulating knowledge. "Too little acknowledgment is afforded to the context brought to the process by the learner" (ibid., p. 12).

We might, therefore, give up on the idea that we can find a methodological framework, or research model, to guide the teaching of research processes. Knowledge-building is, to be sure, an eclectic and multi-party process involving acquiring data and making sense of it, while considering both its biases and ours. So it may well be that defining a single research method is at best artificial and at worst impossible. But the alternative is simply to explain to our students how information works within the discipline and then turn them loose on the tools without giving them any process to follow in moving through their research.

Clearly, many students struggle in the early stages of research projects, not seeing a path ahead and feeling a great deal of anxiety that is not alleviated simply by providing them with a rubber-stamp method (Kuhlthau, 2011). It is a fact, as well, that actual research processes are often cyclical, so that initial information gathered leads to reformulation of the research question/hypothesis, leading to more information gathering and writing, which may cause the researcher to return to the resource acquisition stage to bolster the knowledge base or even back to the hypothesis once again to clarify it. This is particularly true of research scholars, whose methodologies are varied and often appear to have no organized structure (Stoan, 1984). But we do not have sufficient reason to avoid putting the application of whatever research processes we are teaching within a methodological framework. As Bodi (2002) has pointed out, established scholars have a knowledge base that allows for the ambiguities and potential confusion of circular research. University students, having a much less mature knowledge base and, indeed, lacking a coherent sense of the purposes and techniques of the research process, flounder in their research, often rejecting whatever method they have been taught but substituting nothing better. They need a fairly consistent road map.

Bodi argues:

> Librarians tend to teach a step-by-step, linear search strategy, but research, especially in an electronic environment, is interactive and circular. A coherent, flexible research model that can be adapted to various instructional sessions is necessary, but we need to be clear that one strategy does not fit all circumstances. (2002, p. 113)

Without some sort of flexibly conceived framework for research method, any mechanical skills remain orphans, lacking a blueprint to determine when they should be used. The best way to instill a research methodology is to build assignments around a research process, providing examples that indicate when, and in what manner, the researcher will need to deviate from the normal pattern. In this way, students do not just have a set of tools and some skills to use them, but they also have a process by which using the tools can lead to understanding and problem-solving.

There is a time-honored methodology available to us, however, which can answer most of the methodological doubts we have raised to this point. It is the scientific method. Instantly, we can raise a number of objections – the scientific method too is artificial, limits creativity, and is too rationalistic to deal with all the subjectivity involved in turning information into knowledge. But, as a method, it brings together the main features of most problem-solving in the human enterprise – development of a working knowledge of the issue, creation of a statement that crystallizes the nature of problem at hand (hypothesis or research question), a review of what is currently known about the issue (including a delineation of the various points of view that are held), an exercise to compile and/or evaluate evidence, and a conclusion that weighs all that has been discovered and finds a solution. This method can take many views on an issue into account, can properly address the bias brought by the researcher, and can help discern what passes for "information" to determine its quality/usefulness/reliability in helping to deal with the stated problem.

The scientific research model can be pictured simply as shown in Figure 5.1. Figure 5.1 includes the formulation of a question (or hypothesis), data gathering and synthesis, some sort of process of analysis (evaluation), consideration of resulting information, and development of conclusions. As such, it can work in everything from a science project with literature review to a history paper on the role of 9/11 in shaping immigration policy in the early twenty-first century.

Though the actual course of a research project may not be nearly as linear as Figure 5.1 appears to make it (Kulthau, 2011), it at least puts forward an A–Z process to conceptualize and carry out research in a variety of disciplines. For students lacking any real concept of what they are doing or where they are going in research, it can provide a basic roadmap.

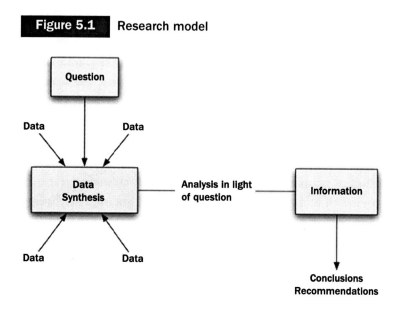

Figure 5.1 Research model

Instruction in application skills

Teaching the application of a research process – how to use keywords and controlled vocabularies; how to search catalogs, databases, and the Internet; how to evaluate information sources – is the predominant territory for many information literacy instructors today. Generally, application is not taught to any great extent by subject faculty members, who leave it for librarians (Bury, 2011). Application skill is important, but as we have argued, it needs to be taught within the spheres of philosophy of information (epistemology) and use a flexible research method if students are to bear fruit in the effective acquiring and use of information.

To use an analogy, the application of research is like a tradesperson's skill with his or her tools. Proper use of the tools is not enough if the tradesperson has not been educated in the engineering and regulatory aspects of the trade and has not developed expertise in using the right tool to accomplish each stage of the task with skill.

Elmborg wrote:

> If literacy is the ability to read, interpret, and produce texts valued in a community, then academic information literacy is the ability to read, interpret, and produce information valued in academia – a skill that must be developed by all students during their college education ... Students must learn how information functions in proof or argument, and why that information is accepted while other information is not. Ultimately, students need to produce information that meets the community's standards ... Information literacy, seen in this way, is more than a set of acquired skills. It involves the comprehension of an entire system of thought and the ways that information flows in that system. Ultimately, it also involves the capacity to critically evaluate the system itself. (2006, p. 196)

This requires more than remedial library instruction. It must encompass a comprehensive program of student development. Now is the time to get the teaching of research processes firmly on the academic map, with a level of credibility that will be unassailable. There is certainly enough literature available to prepare us for the teaching task and there are sufficient teachers, if they are equipped, supported and motivated. If there are inadequacies in any aspect, they can be overcome. But we absolutely must take teaching research processes as seriously as do any other foundational aspect of higher education.

To make research processes instruction work, it has to find a home within the curriculum, not as an elective, nor as one program among many, but as an element of the core of every student's education. As such, it will take a variety of forms and venues from stand-alone courses in majors to through-the-curriculum credit-bearing modules within existing courses. But to make it anything less than a core goal is to leave our students unprepared for the information age.

Metanarrative as a way of conceptualizing research processes

There is one idea that pulls together philosophy, methodology and application within the disciplines: the concept of *metanarrative*. The term "metanarrative" is unfamiliar to some and highly controversial to others, thus calling for another brief foray into philosophy.

It is a truism that practice arises out of philosophy and that practice divorced from philosophy is often half-blown and less than helpful. This is certainly the case in the realm of research processes instruction, where a tendency to move to the pragmatic before we know why and what we are doing often fragments our endeavors into a wide variety of disparate initiatives, few of which accomplish any more than a small part of the task. The philosophical concept of "metanarrative" can bring cohesion to our efforts to create a rigorous plan for teaching research processes within disciplines.

The term "metanarrative" itself is not particularly mysterious. Our daily lives are filled with a series of "narratives" – how we got to work this morning, how we handled a particular situation, how we decided what to have for lunch, and so on. Binding our smaller narratives together is one or more *metanarratives*, that is, larger explanations of our reality that guide us through our smaller narratives. Metanarrative explains in big picture fashion why we do what we do and thus defines our view of the world or a portion of it.

To consider an example, those who teach research processes believe that enabling students to handle information skillfully is an essential element of their education and must be pursued vigorously. That is an example of a metanarrative. It is a guiding belief or consensus that helps us set our educational goals and provides the rationale for doing what we do. Thus, a metanarrative is both a motivator and a way of measuring the "truth" or validity of what we are doing. Capitalism is a metanarrative for business and economics, as is, alternatively, socialism. Scientific method is the metanarrative for experimentation in the sciences. Religions are metanarratives for individual lives of faith.

With the rise of Postmodernism, the concept of a metanarrative, as an embracing explanation or rationale for why we do what we do, has come under attack. French philosopher Jean-François Lyotard (1984), and Michael Peters (1995) from the field of education, among many others, have argued that the idea of a metanarrative cannot stand as a philosophical or even a practical concept because there are too many diverse metanarratives to allow for consensus on much of anything. To say that a discipline uses a certain method to discuss issues and advance knowledge is to fly against the reality that there are multiple methods in every discipline. What is more, they argue, there is no consensus about how any academic enterprise is to be furthered, and if there were such a consensus, there would be no way of determining whether it was more "true" than some other possible consensus.

If, indeed, metanarrative is a useless concept, then we have little to talk about. But Postmodernism, focusing on subjectivity and rejection of the rationalistic idea of truth, has in recent years increasingly been losing its own credibility.

In many ways it has always been a philosophical concept rather than a practical reality, a Western luxury embraced by we who have most of our daily needs met and can afford to speculate on our diversity rather than clinging to our commonality. While Postmodernism has well taught us that we are all essentially subjective beings whose personal experiences color all that we see and do, it has failed to recognize that in the real world we must live by consensus to survive.

While it is easy to make the case that each of us is subjective, so that coming to a consensus/metanarrative about why and how we do things is rarely possible and is probably invalid if we do so, the fact is that we all, in the practical world, live by consensus. Traffic in our streets flows well (with some exceptions) because we agree on what the rules are, even when there are no police officers nearby. Written communication is possible because we agree on the symbolic meaning of letters, definitions of words, and grammatical structures of sentences. Thus in the face of Postmodern criticism, we can continue to affirm the reality of metanarratives that guide the way in which we function, do our disciplines, and so on.

Let's bring this down to the task of teaching research processes. We are arguing that we must move away from our often fragmented approaches and enlist the aid of metanarratives based on the way scholars in disciplines actually think about and perform research to further knowledge.

Disciplines in the academic world each carry something of a consensus about the way to "do" that discipline. In fact, disciplines themselves are defined as much by their beliefs, values and agreed-upon methods as they are by their subject matter. While disagreements arise (some of them heated), discipline practitioners tend to work out their problems and maintain their consensus about the best ways to do their work, or else they form separate schools of thought, each with its own consensus. But the affirmation continues that there is a consensus about why and how to do things, or a "metanarrative" of the discipline. It is obvious that there is no single metanarrative in any discipline. Different scholars approach their work in different ways. Some are conservative, while others are radical, constantly pushing the boundaries. But this in no way negates the fact that disciplines have overarching conventions, consistent ways in which they live and advance, based upon what they commonly value and believe.

All of this serves to make a crucial point – the teaching of research processes works best when it is structured within the idea of a metanarrative. Even when we move in "interdisciplinary" directions, there are metanarratives that define what we are trying to accomplish and identify methods that will succeed better than will others.

Learning about versus doing

There is a tendency in higher education, models of which date back to the time of the Renaissance, to see the educational task as passing the knowledge of the expert down to the novice. Thus we continue to promote the lecture, which some wag long ago described as the transmission of information from the professor's notes to the student's notes without passing through the mind of either.

The lecture, as the primary mode of education, has come under attack in recent decades for perpetuating a false notion of what it means to be educated. Those who teach at university level are likely well aware of the arguments against it: students retain more by "active learning," while the lecture is essentially a "passive" exercise; the lecture exacerbates the idea of a large distinction between expert and novice, as if only experts really know things; students these days demand engagement, which they don't find in a lecture, and so on. Likely, the lecture itself will never die as one means among many to educate, but it has certainly been challenged.

What is not often stated, however, is that the lecture, when used exclusively, creates a distance between the learner and the subject matter. The exclusively lecturing professor is saying something like this to the student: "This subject matter is my territory. I will pass some of my knowledge onto you, but please do not dare to believe that what you hear makes you an expert. My task is to teach you *about* my subject matter, not to enable you to do what I can do with it. I am the expert and only I can truly *do* this discipline. You are not part of my academic social circle, which cost me so much time and energy to enter and inhabit."

On at least two levels, such a message accords with the realities of academic life. First, the very essence of expertise appears to be its distinction from lack of expertise. We value our experts precisely because they are *not* like us. If they were like us, they wouldn't be experts, would they? Academia, in fact, has a strongly vested interest in perpetuating expertise as the primary reason for its being. A professor is a professor because he/she knows and does things that set them apart to be able to teach others.

The tendency, therefore, in many institutions of higher learning is to teach students *about* the disciplines, assuming that they will remain outsiders until they have paid the same dues their professors have done, in the trenches of comprehensive exams and dissertations. Like a walled community of elites, we guard our expertise, not imparting any more of it than we have to, for fear that the masses may end up wandering our streets and spoiling our exclusivity. This may seem extreme, but it spells out at least one reason why students tend to learn *about* disciplines rather than learning to enter into and actually to *do* disciplines, at least until they reach Master's and doctoral programs.

A second reason rests in the reality that students lack the knowledge to be genuine disciplinarians like us. Would we really want an undergraduate, or even a beginning graduate, student to be messing around in primary sources or doing actual original experiments? When it does happen, we are generally fairly paternalistic about the outcome, seeing it as a mimicking of genuine research rather than research itself. How can students be expected actually to *do* a discipline when they are outsiders trying to get in but lacking the qualifications to do so?

Thus our carefully guarded expertise and our limited opinion of student abilities tend to keep students on the outside of our disciplines, where they learn *about* the subject matter and imitate some of the method but never actually enter into the heart of what it means to be an actual disciplinarian. Perhaps there will always be some such barriers, but, if we are seeking skilled student researchers, we need to get past these limitations, to stop protecting our turf so strongly, and to believe that genuine research rather than pale imitation is both possible from students, and necessary.

The difference between disciplinary experts and undergraduates

It is a long process from the first undergraduate year at university to completion of a Ph.D. and entrance into a teaching and research post of one's own. One can scarcely recall any longer what it was like to be that entering undergraduate walking with trepidation into Dr. Smith's philosophy course for the first time. One can hardly remember that first chemistry laboratory assignment, when nothing worked the way the manual said it should, and the fear of humiliation was a constant companion.

But that's just the point. We scarcely recall what was like to be an undergraduate. Probably it was frightening, but we were bright and motivated young people who coped and learned and eventually triumphed over whatever adversity was besetting us. True, we were probably more intelligent than many of our class members, but, frankly, a lot of them seemed unmotivated and confused. They lacked our skills and our drive. Now these former fellow students are merely part of our dim past because few, if any, of them actually went on to doctoral studies like we did.

We have become experts, defined by our degrees and publications, as well as, hopefully, our track record for imparting our knowledge to appreciative students. We believe we are doing a good job of teaching, though student research projects seem shabby in contrast to the sorts of things we produced when we were undergraduates (hindsight tending to cast a golden hue over everything). Students, in fact, seem somewhat baffled by our directions to them regarding these projects, no matter how carefully we formulate our wording. What is so difficult, for goodness sake, about developing one of seven possible topics, finding a mere eight to ten references from scholarly sources (at least three of these being journal articles), and writing a project, using a good dose of critical thinking? Any one of us could produce a 3,000-word paper of this type in a few days, with all of our references cited in flawless style.

What, then, is going through the head of the typical undergraduate or even the head of someone in the first year of graduate study? You might be surprised. I am reminded of the famous Far Side cartoon where the dog Ginger's master is berating her about something. He thinks he is being perfectly clear, but all she hears is "Blah, blah, blah, Ginger, blah, Ginger, blah, blah, Ginger." The difference between a disciplinary expert and an undergraduate is more than a distinction in level of knowledge. The two are actually living in different worlds using different languages.

Librarians are in a unique position to observe the communication problem, and those of us who are academic reference librarians encounter it constantly:

Student: Professor Smith wants 3,000 words on 1930s Marxism at Cambridge University.

Librarian: Do you have some sense of how you are supposed to address the topic?

Student: With at least five books and three journal articles.

Librarian: What have you done so far?

Student: Wikipedia article on Cambridge U. It didn't have anything I can use and Dr. Smith hates Wikipedia anyway.

Librarian: What course does Dr. Smith teach?

Student: European politics.

Librarian: Did he tell you what the goal of the project was? What does he expect you to accomplish?

Student: To write about Marxists at the University of Cambridge. Explain about them.

And so on. The student clearly thinks the goal is to find out what she or he can about these Marxists and then write it out. The professor, who is calling for critical thinking, is seeking some sort of analysis of the role of these Marxists, or of their importance within European political movements of the era, or whatever. It seems so obvious that this is a rich topic for cutting-edge critical thinking (perhaps even an analysis of the fascinating influence of former Cambridge student Kim Philby in contributing to the politics of the Cold War). Yet the student seems primed to regurgitate sources, re-describe what is already known, and show little to no use of critical thinking processes. There is no sense that there actually is a goal to the project other than explaining the facts.

What went wrong? This student, while she or he can study up on the topic, has little sense of how such a topic is to be addressed. She or he has no grasp of the purposes of political historical research, let alone understanding which research resources are best and most suited to addressing those purposes. She or he is an outsider in a field Dr Smith thinks of as his own. This student is not part of the academy and, despite the requirement to do this research project, she or he has not been invited into the inner sanctum where the real researchers do their work. Not only does she or he not understand historical/political method, but she or he has no sense of the metanarrative that any self-respecting political historian lives by. This is an alien world in which "research" sounds like blah, blah, blah, and the only recourse is to find some data on the topic and summarize it.

Bright students regularly and persistently draw a blank when it comes to following the directions provided for research projects. According to Head (2008), simply identifying what the professor wants is the primary challenge among students. Somehow they are not understanding our directions, perhaps in the same way that the Far Side's Ginger only hears her name and not the rest of the rebuke. Experts and undergraduates live in different worlds with different metanarratives expressed in different languages. To assume that an undergraduate is going to take our vague command for good research and critical thinking, and run with it, is to risk almost constant disappointment. There is too much that needs to be known about doing a discipline, requiring knowledge and skill that the average student does not possess.

The radical shift in thinking demanded for effective research processes instruction to university students

If we want our students to be skilled researchers, which they certainly need to be to address the ever increasing demands of our information age, we are going to need to rethink education. Some may argue that we have already done so with the development of active learning and constructivist pedagogies intended to put learning into the hands of students. The lecture as the primary form of educating may not be dead, but there is much more of an emphasis on student learning than professorial teaching. Surely that must be good for education. And it is.

But something is missing. Essentially, it is a lack of a conceptualization of the means we must use to ensure student engagement. What, essentially, are we supposed to do to take the emphasis from professor as teacher to the student as learner? What is the underlying philosophy behind "student as learner"? When we espouse the constructivist notion of students finding their own meaning in the information resources they use, what exactly does that entail? There is much said about active, student-involved learning, and it all sounds very good. Yet there is a foundation that is not being built, a basic understanding about what we are supposed to be doing that eludes us.

Just as our existing notions of teaching research processes are not robust enough, some of our plans for active student learning are generally not well enough defined to make the shift to a new method of teaching student researchers that radical enough to succeed. We must seek a new approach.

6

Research processes in the classroom

Abstract: Research processes instruction does not have to be an intrusion into the classroom but can, in fact, become the foundation of newer educational emphases such as process learning, deep learning, twenty-first-century skills and student self-learning. Within existing models of active learning, however, not enough attention has been paid to how disciplines handle information. There is, also, a lack of perception that student information handling skills remain limited and haphazard without careful and extensive guidance. If students, indeed, are going to be active learners, with their professors providing the expertise of methodology rather than merely dumping content, students are going to have to know how to work with information effectively. In the new classroom, professors will ask themselves, and their students, critical questions about the nature of information in their disciplines and about the ways in which skilled research processes are to be conceptualized.

Key words: active learning, Boyer Commission, constructivism, deep learning, disciplines, heutagogy, process skills, student-centered learning.

There is a great distinction between a basic orientation to library resources and genuine instruction in research processes. With the majority of information research instruction now focused on one-shot sessions, we have seen that our students are not being prepared for the information age. If we can agree that more is needed, the burning question becomes, "How do we help our students to become skilled researchers?"

Essential goals

It is best first to identify the essence of what we are looking for. Here is a summary of the key criteria for persons with high ability in research processes: We want students who have a knowledgeable facility with various types of information and who feel comfortable with identifying a research problem, acquiring relevant information from a variety of sources, evaluating what they have found, and applying it to the problem at hand. We do not want clumsy, barely adequate information handlers. We want people who are able researchers.

Still, the effort of primarily academic librarians to teach research processes continues to be viewed by many professors as an intrusion into academia. It need not be. This chapter will contend that research processes instruction can, in fact, become the *foundation* for some of the most exciting trends in higher education today – those related to educational emphases such as process learning, deep learning, twenty-first-century skills and student self-learning. Let's turn to these newer movements now.

Congruence with active learning and constructivism

Discussion of today's higher education is increasingly permeated by an emphasis on process learning as opposed to mere content learning. This distinction is, perhaps, unfortunate in that the assimilation of content must always be part of the requirement of the student's educational experience and even seemingly "pure" content has an admixture of process within it.

Perhaps we would do better to distinguish between passive and active learning. In the new information environment, we are discovering that content by itself is a cheap commodity. Dare we say it, a student could become immersed in Wikipedia for a year and emerge speaking and acting like a college graduate. Perhaps the knowledge base would be shallow, and the experience with actually doing a discipline would be weak, but there would be sufficient ingrained content to fool many of us. Content has become cheap, and practices that merely transfer content from information source (professor or textual material) to student are losing their significance, because they embody passive learning only.

In this current educational environment, active learning initiatives, intended to focus less on information dissemination and more on student learning, are gaining credibility in academia, though the jury is still out on whether active learning is advancing at the same pace as is the cheapening of mere content. Gilchrist (2007) summarizes variations of process (active) learning as follows:

Problem-based learning in which students identify issues and use existing and acquired knowledge to address them.

Inquiry-based learning in which students rather than instructors pose a series of questions which they then address with existing or acquired knowledge.

Resource/Research-based learning in which students learn through resources and their own research so that the professor is a guide rather than an information disseminator.

Project-based learning in which students package the research they do in the form of project reports.

While it is obvious that these various forms of learning overlap, they represent some common, but certainly not all, current approaches to active learning.

At their extremes, the two main approaches to education are teacher-centered instruction, and what Hase and Kenyon (2000, 2007) called heutagogy or student self-learning. The former is characterized by lectures and other forms of information dissemination. The latter puts the responsibility for learning into the hands of the student. Hase and Kenyon write: "A heutagogical approach recognises the need to be flexible in the learning where the teacher provides resources but the learner designs the actual course he or she might take by negotiating the learning" (2000, p. 6).

If research processes instruction were built into heutagogy, the professor would be providing tools for discovery, and the student would learn by identifying research problems of various sorts, acquiring needed information, and then evaluating and using that information effectively to address those identified problems.

There are several challenges, however, to the possibility of education done on the extreme edge of the student-centered approach:

- With responsibility for learning in the hands of students, we need to question whether or not these naïve learners will have a sufficient knowledge base in order to work effectively with the resources they are discovering. E.D. Hirsch (2006), in particular, has cautioned that reading and critical thinking skills only function well when they are founded on a solid base of knowledge.

- It's not clear that students will warm easily to a "guide on the side" approach to education. Many, if not most, students are uncertain as they move through the subject matter of their education, and they look to their professors to mark the signposts and help them make the journey.

- Some disciplines appear highly resistant to student-directed learning, particularly those like the sciences and law, which demand a considerable amount of factual knowledge before method can be engaged effectively (Carpenter and Tait, 2001).

We are left with a dilemma. The new information age, on the one hand, has made information an increasingly cheap commodity, and the traditional lecture method is to a large extent an anachronism based in an era when the educated elite possessed the knowledge base and passed it on to the select few. Active learning and student-centered methods seem to be the best alternative. On the other hand, making students totally responsible for their own learning creates problems arising from their need for a knowledge base and their uncertainty about method as they proceed through uncharted subject matter.

The literature regarding these issues is enormous, and we can only deal with a fraction of it. One promising area of study is that of "deep" versus "surface" learning, pioneered by Marton and Säljö (1976a, 1976b) and Svensson (1977). Marton and Säljö tested various types of retention of article content read by subjects, determining that some of their subjects processed information superficially, recalling the facts but failing to show deeper understanding of the purposes of the articles read. That is, surface learners learned the sign (what is actually written) while deep learners learned what it signified. Svensson (1977) characterized these two approaches to learning as atomistic (focusing on details) and holistic (focusing on meaning). What is more, these researchers found that there was a connection between students' views of what was expected of them and the ways in which they processed the information they were reading (Marton and Säljö, 1976b).

Following on the work of Marston, Säljö and Svensson, Biggs (1979) discovered that students who were told that credit would be given for factual recall adjusted their study methods for recall, which was detrimental to overall understanding and critique of written material. Students who were told that credit would be given for understanding and higher order thinking adjusted their study methods to achieve that task.

Atherton (2010) argues that deep learning is that which ties learning with practice in such a way that the student is "making sense" or "comprehending the world by re-interpreting knowledge." At its most basic level, "surface learning" is merely the acquisition and retention of knowledge, while "deep learning" involves understanding the subject matter in a way that makes sense of it and uses existing knowledge as a tool to advance beyond mere rote learning. (In other contexts, this sort of deep learning would be discussed using the terminology of constructivism.)

Thus, while professors may not be able totally to overcome student tendencies to work primarily to meet the requirements of an assignment or an exam, it is possible to alter learning approaches by making deep learning the intended goal of instruction and informing students of the requirements to achieve success in such an environment.

We have not yet, however, identified research processes ability within active learning initiatives. A significant step forward in this regard is found in the Boyer Commission and its descendants. The Boyer Commission Report (Kenny, 1998) looked into the education of undergraduates at major research universities, arguing that research universities must make inquiry-based learning the foundational pattern so that the focus is on undergraduates observing, doing, and communicating research under the direction of senior researchers. While burdened by a measure of elitism, in that there is no reason why non-research universities could not move in similar directions given adequate support, the Boyer Report has become the basis for advances being made on a number of fronts, as, for example, the University of California, Berkeley, and its Undergraduate Student Learning Initiative (*http://vpapf.chance.berkeley.edu/usli.htm*).

The Boyer Report has more recently been followed up by a large study entitled *Developing Undergraduate Research and Inquiry* (Healey and Jenkins, 2009), which calls for all students, not just an elite few, to be engaged with research. There are four ways to do this:

> *research-led*: learning about current research in the discipline;
>
> *research-oriented*: developing research skills and techniques;
>
> *research-based*: undertaking research and inquiry;
>
> *research-tutored*: engaging in research discussions.
>
> (ibid., p. 6)

While all four approaches are valid and are often interlinked, the authors favor the latter two, which involve students directly in the research process. With regard to teaching students how to function within disciplines, Healey and Jenkins write:

> Engaging students in undergraduate research and inquiry is one of the most effective ways to help students to begin to think like a chemist, historian or engineer,

> which arguably is one of the core graduate attributes for most discipline-based degree programmes ... Moreover, there is strong evidence that students involved in research-based inquiries develop more sophisticated levels of intellectual development. (ibid., p. 49)

The case studies provided by Healey and Jenkins do reveal elements of inquiry-based learning, but most of the described initiatives encompass only a few elements of their four-part emphasis, and there is a persistent sense that something is missing. While the idea of engaging students in research is an excellent one, there is a general neglect in such initiatives of the foundational element of such research – the ability to handle information skillfully within a disciplinary framework, in which the professor constantly guides students as they acquire and use information to solve problems.

There is indeed a growing literature dealing with teaching students how to function as scholars within disciplines. The disciplinary framework is seen as a key venue within which information work (research) is done, so understanding how disciplines work to advance knowledge is often seen as a key element of active/process learning (for example, Ding, 2008; Dressen-Hammouda, 2008; Riordan, 2008; Caccavo, 2009).

Where many such initiatives, whether Boyer, Healey and Jenkins, or the discipline-focused "teach them how to be scientists" fall down, however, is in two related areas – not enough attention is being paid to how disciplines handle information, and there is a lack of perception that student information handling skills remain limited and haphazard without careful and extensive instruction. We now turn to these issues.

Required thinking and process skills

The idea of teaching students to think along disciplinary lines, coming to grasp what makes a discipline "tick," is not new to higher education. But the foundational role of the teaching of research processes, with an emphasis on information handling, is scarcely on the horizon in studies of disciplinary instruction. One that has come close, however, is Carter (2007) who enlisted the aid of student outcomes to demonstrate that faculty-determined disciplinary skills can form the basis for teaching students how to function well within disciplines. Many of the program outcome statements in his study had elements related to research processes – ability to identify research problems, acquire information, evaluate it critically, write papers that effectively address research problems, and so on.

Carter argued that disciplines need to be seen as "active ways of knowing" (ibid., p. 387). He identified four meta-genres of academic work that reflect four broad approaches to disciplines. They are: (1) academic work that calls for problem solving; (2) empirical enquiry; (3) research from sources; and (4) performance. Approaches like Carter's can go a long way toward identifying the kinds of abilities required in information handling within disciplines.

Nichols has argued:

> The most important task of an undergraduate student is to learn to be a member of a disciplinary community, to tap into the knowledge and practice embodied in the community. Her path will take her from somewhere outside the discipline to a place inside. (2009, p. 528)

This, as Nichols makes plain, is an extension of the work of Brown, Collins, and Duguid (1989) who argued that the artificial separation in much of education of "know what" from "know how" misses the point that cognition is situated in a context that gives it meaning. Knowledge is like language. Just as a definition does not truly capture the meaning of a word out of context, so knowledge is defined contextually. Academic disciplines, like workplaces, are cultures or communities within which knowledge is not static but is actually something being *done*. Learning is intended to acculturate the student within the context of that knowledge, that is, within "authentic activities," defined as "the ordinary practices of the culture" (ibid., p. 34). Students thus learn within "cognitive apprenticeships."

What may we conclude? We live in an era in which information is a cheap commodity, and simply disseminating it is having less and less of an academic value in the classroom. The actual significance of today's professor is his/her expertise in handing the hows and whys of the discipline. Thus, the focus is moving from the data to the metanarrative, from what we need to know to how we work, in a disciplinary context, with what we know.

We see it in many forms today – constructivism (students finding their own meaning), deep learning, self-learning, active learning, situated learning, and twenty-first-century skills. There is a growing consensus that, while it will always be important to know things, the educated person of the future needs the skills of critical thinking, ability to work with data in problem-solving, and adaptability to new situations. This is the territory of disciplinary metanarrative – the area of hows and whys more than of the whats.

Does a professor, then, still have anything to offer in today's information-saturated world? Yes. Professors have expertise, that amazing ability to guide students, to help them navigate through the subject matter, especially through the problem-solving and critical thinking skills that make the discipline work. The professor is not merely an information dispensing machine but a skilled navigator of a complex landscape. This emphasis on expert navigation will need to become our priority as educators if we do not want to become anachronisms. And if students, indeed, are going to be active learners, with their professors providing the expertise of methodology rather than merely dumping content, students are going to have to know how to work with information effectively.

I find a great uneasiness in higher education today. Old ways, which have persisted since the Renaissance, no longer work well. Our students are lost in Google and Wikipedia, and we are hard-pressed to get them back to our books and journals that seem so archaic to them. Mere lectures no longer do the job and everywhere there's a call for new methods that focus on learning. The existing research is virtually unanimous in saying that active learning works better than passive learning.

Meanwhile, the workplace is playing an ever-increasing role in determining what is important in education. A survey done on behalf of the Association of American Colleges and Universities (Hart Research Associates, 2010) found that only 25 percent of employers believed that American two- and four-year colleges were doing a good job of preparing students for the global economy. Most employers called for a more sophisticated ability to deal with complex situations and adapt current knowledge to new environments. Very highly rated skills were critical thinking, problem-solving, efficient information acquisition from multiple sources, and effective collaboration. These are also the very elements most prized in teaching research processes.

One body of academics needs to be enlisted, however, if we are to make a success of such teaching – the librarians. A new form of cooperative teaching is required, calling for faculty members to see academic librarians in a new light. Why? Because the primary tool of active learning is the ability to handle the information base well. Professors have a good grasp of the metanarratives of disciplines. The information skills of disciplines, however – identifying problems to solve, effectively and efficiently finding the best and most relevant information, evaluating that information and applying it well to the problem at hand – are skills requiring the active participation of information specialists, primarily academic librarians.

Information specialists understand the whole sweep of the information world, both traditional and non-traditional, the complex tools of today's information acquisition, and the information handling skills required in today's information age. Professors understand the nuances of their disciplines. Together, professors and academic librarians can make the teaching of research processes more robust than ever imagined, and more foundational to the education process itself.

Required changes in teaching patterns

How did most academics initially become experts in their fields? Not by spending time memorizing details, though that did happen, but by *experiencing* the subject matter, working with it, debating its findings, testing it, and connecting with others who had varying views about it.

Expertise is not the same as knowledge. Expertise is knowledge on a mission, knowledge in action. The expert disciplinarian does not merely have knowledge. The expert *does* knowledge. Thus, instructing students to know the facts and variants of our disciplines without an emphasis on learning how to *do* our disciplines seems to be a less than viable educational plan.

Yet, the traditional primacy of content over method in most disciplines is a strong barrier to active learning initiatives. The mantra, "I have barely enough time to cover the content as it is," becomes an impetus to maintain the lecture as the preferred mode of teaching, and student notes as the preferred method of preparing for the exam, which measures content absorption more than ability to work with the knowledge base critically. Method thus becomes a by-product rather than a central focus of our educational plan. While program goals may include critical thinking and research skills, these are the least likely to be assessed if they are not deliberately taught. Many professors simply assume that method will follow content, like a puppy following its master. It won't.

It's tempting at this point to use a cliché along the lines of, "A thousand-mile journey begins with a single step." Yet it may well be the most appropriate advice to offer at this point. Turning a content-oriented classroom into an exercise in critical thinking and doing of the discipline is certainly not a transformation that can be made all at once. It requires both the will of all the players and the expertise of both subject specialists and information professionals.

I am convinced that this both can and must happen, simply because all the goalposts have moved with the dawn of the information age. Students now can get their information from anywhere they wish. They don't need knowledge pushers. They need knowledge guides.

Where the current active learning movement in education has gone wrong is in failing to recognize that the ability to handle information in a highly technological information environment is foundational, not remedial. The teaching of research processes, in fact, can in itself form the basis for new patterns of education that are active, inductive, and problem-based. If the goal of the new education is to teach students how to think for themselves, then they need to know how to enlist critical analysis to work through the issues of a discipline until they become skilled disciplinarians. In this context, research processes instruction is right there, saying, "I can do that." All of the goals of a new active, constructivist educational philosophy are the goals of ability with research processes.

Let us, then, consider the initial steps for a research processes-based higher education. A good place to start with helping students to grasp the nature of disciplinary thinking is, perhaps surprisingly, autobiography. A professor who begins a new course with a narrative about how he or she came to be there teaching that particular class can be both interesting and instructive. What motivates you to be devoted to this discipline? What were your own struggles (if you can remember them) as you made the transition from outsider to insider? Who are your disciplinary heroes and what were the grand ideas for which they were known? How did you learn the method of your discipline, and what were some of the mistakes you made along the way? Autobiography can be a first foray into the concept that disciplines are as much a process as a body of knowledge.

There are other questions to ask as we prepare to teach research processes within our course instruction. To prime the pump on disciplinary thinking processes, let me pose several of these that a professor could ask and answer in order to tune in to disciplinary process thinking.

Why does this discipline exist?

Not only does this question speak to the importance of the discipline, but also to its place within the hierarchy of knowledge and to the methodology that gives it its importance. The justification of the existence of a discipline goes a long way toward spelling out both its importance and its function.

Where does its knowledge base come from?

Different disciplines draw from different sources of information, and, indeed, value certain types of information over other types. In asking a question about knowledge base, we are considering the necessary information foundation upon which the discipline relies (epistemology).

What must be included in this discipline's knowledge base?

When we begin to consider essentials, that is, the knowledge that a discipline simply cannot do without, we learn a great deal about what the disciplinary priorities are. Interestingly, all disciplines include within their knowledge bases bodies of information that the discipline would label foundational or even factual. This is information that has little controversy attached to it but is a solid, well-rooted deposit passed on from generation to generation, growing and perhaps changing slowly over time. All disciplines thus place a high value on student assimilation of core information and acceptance of that information as a given. Beyond that, all disciplines value the more cutting-edge information that still resides in the realm of investigation, discovery and analysis.

Why and how is academic discourse carried out as it is in this discipline?

What is so important about the way this discipline "does things"? Students commonly believe that only their professors understand the ground rules, the methodology that makes one an insider in the discipline. When the approach to academic discourse is a mystery, the student remains an outsider. When students begin to learn the insider assumptions, requirements and methodological "rules," they are much more likely to want to be insiders themselves.

Why does this discipline argue and use evidence as it does? What constitutes good evidence and what does not?

Once we have determined that the approach of the discipline is justifiable, we need to look at how the discipline ensures that its knowledge base is built on reliable evidence. Not to grasp what constitutes legitimate evidence in a discipline is to miss a basic plank of that discipline's ethos. When students understand the ground rules of academic argumentation and evidence, this understanding is like gold.

How does this discipline determine which scholars will be its major players?

Every discipline has its movers and shakers, its go-to people for the best research and writing in the field. By what criteria do these scholars gain this kind of recognition? Even given that we can spell out the criteria, we may have to explain the landscape of the dissenters in the discipline or the conflicting schools of thought that have formed within it. Thus there is an intellectual geography to every discipline that shapes it and governs its developing tenets. Student insiders will need to understand that landscape.

The new classroom

The point of beginning our courses with an analysis and explanation of disciplinary thinking is to enable the student to enter the world of the disciplinarian and to understand the process, not simply the content, of the discipline. Not only is this a good approach simply from the standpoint of inviting students into an understanding of a discipline's inner working, but it is absolutely essential to helping students to become good researchers within it. As information itself becomes a cheap commodity, helping students to become disciplinarians, to do the discipline and generate research within it, needs to be central to the future of academic instruction.

The new classroom needs to be much more a laboratory than a place for content assimilation. Content can often be learned just as easily through readings and short lectures, while the majority of time in the classroom can be focused on method. This should involve close reading in class of key standard works, or portions of them, an emphasis on the main ideas and key scholars, and a strong dose of hands-on practice of the discipline, whether that is analysis and critique of particular approaches, creation of research projects, or introduction of students to the inner workings of their professor's own research.

I do not see a lot of reflection on method among academics, because it is so intuitive to them. But the question of how one gets from problem to solution in a discipline, through a maze of competing voices or evidence, is a crucial one to students, who have not had the time to make the process intuitive. Disciplinary thinking does, obviously, overlap with method, but the latter is more hands-on and gets to the heart of the actual doing of research within a discipline. Thus, teaching research processes as a combination of disciplinary thinking and method can form a foundation for helping students to do the discipline.

Here are some key method questions:

What does the literature in this field actually look like?

Academics are prone to using a combination of lectures and textbooks to impart content, but students generally find themselves as outsiders learning *about* the discipline rather than participating in it. One key way to combine the need for content with an introduction to method is to spend time doing close reading of significant works of actual research, showing how the author developed the thesis or research question, how opposing viewpoints were handled, what was considered evidence and how it was defended, and so on. In the social sciences and sciences, the literature review has great significance, but many students have no idea how to do one. To study literature reviews closely is not only to provide students with content, but to help them begin understanding method – what are the big questions? how are they expressed? what does good critique look like? how do we move from review to advancement of our own hypothesis? and so on.

How does one formulate a viable research question or thesis in this discipline?

The majority of initial "research" done by students consists of compiling data around a topic and then summarizing it without posing a problem or issue. This, of course, is not what disciplinary thinking is about. Reporting on existing knowledge is not research. But students are often baffled by what constitutes a proper research project, as opposed to what they are currently doing. Comments like, "More critical thinking required," or "This paper lacks originality," provide little or no guidance to the student. Disciplinary instruction shows students how the discipline advances by asking certain kinds of questions (hypotheses, problem statements, research questions, or whatever) that lead to the enlistment of data in a problem-solving exercise intended to bring the scholar closer to a solution or an advancement in understanding.

This "information as tool" concept is at the heart of most disciplines (Badke, 2010a). In itself, the concept may not be clear to students, but an additional layer of confusion comes from the varying ways in which a question should be posed, depending upon which discipline you are working with.

Professors, who see the posing of hypotheses, problem statements or research questions as second nature, may well miss the reality that their students lack the experience to set up a viable research proposal or even to see information as a tool rather than as a goal (problem-solving rather than compilation). Disciplinary instruction calls upon professors to revisit the way students formulate research agendas, as well as the criteria that make such agendas either fail or succeed.

How does one determine what sorts of data will be required to address the question or thesis?

Useful data types for one discipline are seen as useless in another. For example, biochemistry sees little value in anecdotal or observational data outside of a rigorous experimental or observational procedure, whereas the views of a newspaper editorial from 1864 may be seen as gold for an American history researcher considering some aspect of the latter days of the Civil War.

When a discipline poses a question or makes a problem statement, it then has to address the sorts of data that will be required to deal with the issue. For novice students it may not be obvious that a statement like, "Scholar X says this and scholar Y says that, but in my opinion . . ." may not have any validity at all. For every discipline, clarifying to students what is considered valid, evidential data, and what is not, is an essential task. Whether it comes from peer-reviewed experimental research in the sciences or convincing evidence supported by several major scholars in the humanities, students need to know what content will work and what will not when addressing an issue.

This calls upon professors to rethink how students should be determining the validity of data in their disciplines, again something that is often intuitive but needs to be developed clearly as an active part of student education. Establishing sets of criteria, providing examples of good and unacceptable data/evidence, and showing what sorts of arguments or conclusions work, and what don't, will go a long way toward enabling students to understand the ground rules.

How does one best acquire the data, using tools that are usually electronic and often complex?

This is a realm where academic librarians can be of immense help, but it may be profitable, not just to invite a librarian into the classroom for an hour, but to collaborate with a librarian to improve your own understanding of relevant databases and to discuss together ways in which the task of searching for resources can be optimized. Resource acquisition is not an isolated task but is closely related to the definition of research problems and to evaluation and use of the resources found. Librarians think about all of these issues constantly. Academic librarians are, in essence, process experts. While they may not have the same deep disciplinary knowledge that you possess, they can help you think about the search process as part of a larger whole.

For example, students who formulate inadequate research questions or theses (too broad, too vague, and so on) will have great difficulty identifying relevant resources. Students who have little grasp of the nature of the literature within a discipline will struggle to evaluate found resources with regard to quality and reliability. When use of research tools is viewed as only one portion of the entire research process, we add depth and rigor to the teaching of research processes.

How does one evaluate and organize the evidence to help it address the research problem?

Accumulated data require sense-making skills on two fronts – determining what is reliable/significant/relevant and organizing the data into a structure that is manageable so that it can be used to address the issue at hand. For the former, evaluation skills are required, but we cannot assume that the average student has them in significant measure. How do I look at a document and determine whether or not it will be of value to the research project I am doing? How do I determine whether or not it will be recognized as high quality scholarship?

For most students, the evaluation and organization of data are a relatively blind process of taking your best guess and hoping it will work out. Solid criteria and guidelines would go a long way toward students being able to assess and use their data well on their own.

What about content?

The mantra most heard from professors considering an active learning approach in their courses is: "But I have to cover the course material." The most efficient (though not always most effective) way to cover course content is simply to lecture. With the lecture, you can plan to cover a certain amount each class (even allowing for a few questions) so that nothing has been missed of the entire content by the end of the semester.

We know, however, the following realities:

- Students retain less of lectures than they do of information they have discovered for themselves.

- Students who actually work with the information, whether researching issues within it or teaching it to others, tend to retain more of what they deal with than if they simply discovered it.

- The goal at the end of the teaching process is to have students who have a reasonably strong knowledge base but also know how to update that knowledge base by working the discipline effectively.

- Ultimately, the content of a course is of little significance if a student is still unable to optimize the knowledge skills of the discipline – the ability to pose problems, determine the best information needed, locate that information, and evaluate it well before putting it to good use.

A knowledge base is necessary, but students increasingly can acquire content on their own. They have less need these days for talking heads and much more need for professors with the expertise to show them how to *do* this thing called a "discipline." At the heart of doing a discipline is teaching students how to handle information within it. Research processes, when taught well, become foundational to content assimilation and to disciplinary thinking and activity. If we worry less about content, finding alternative ways for students to obtain it, and recognize that what students need most is our expertise, we can turn them into skilled researchers and thus skilled disciplinarians.

7

Tentative case studies in disciplinary research process instruction

Abstract: Developing students into skilled researchers begins by inviting them into our disciplines through a merging of content and process within long-term instruction. This involves helping students to understand the knowledge base, metanarrative and method found in each discipline. The chapter suggests ways of approaching instruction regarding these parameters within the humanities, social sciences, sciences and professional programs. Intentionally more suggestive than comprehensive, these suggestions can form the basis for a developed plan to make the teaching of research processes within the disciplines foundational to instruction.

Key words: case studies, humanities, professional programs, sciences, social sciences.

Suggesting practical ways that professors can teach their students is rife with challenges. Professors are disciplinarians, immersed in their subject matter and experienced at doing research in it. For an outsider to their disciplines to suggest better ways of teaching seems both audacious and intrusive. Yet, in what follows, I am not as much trying to interfere as to suggest ways to help professors meet their own goals while at the same time addressing the need of each of their students to become skilled at the research processes cherished in each discipline.

To begin with, a few basic principles may help. First, students need an opportunity to be invited into your discipline. The best way, by far, to do this is to open yourself to them by sharing your own story and your own passions about what you teach. How did you get the "bug" that eventually made you a disciplinary expert? What were the struggles you faced in getting to the inside of your discipline? Who are your disciplinary heroes, and why? What are the grand ideas (comprising your personal metanarrative) that guide your thinking?

Second, you need to begin thinking of your discipline as process, not just content. Where does your knowledge base come from, and by what means? What are the major conventions of presenting data and arguing evidence? How does one determine that the presenting case has been made? How and why do some scholars in the discipline become major players? And so on. It is only when process shares the same stage as content that you have a balanced approach to the discipline. Remember that process is intuitive to you but not to your students. The major barrier to a student actually becoming a disciplinary insider is not so much a lack of knowledge as a lack of understanding of, and ability with, process.

Third, research processes are not taught by brief, remedial instruction but by consistent experiences with observing and doing those processes in a context of instruction and feedback. Think of what is needed to learn a new language, and you will have a sense of the complexity involved and the sheer effort needed to develop skilled researchers. A one-off assignment won't do it.

Fourth, despite their often low level of recognition academically, academic librarians are the process experts on your campus, not in the sense that they know more about process than you do, but that they have *thought* more about process and *done* more actual instruction to students in research processes than have teaching faculty. A good reference or instruction librarian has counseled multiple students in the development of research statements, acquisition of information resources, advancement of ideas, evaluation of found information and presentation of research reports. Librarians think about process all the time, and they need to be considered crucial allies in your own journey into effective teaching of research processes. Few academic librarians bite, and most of them are the most giving, self-effacing people you will meet. In the examples that follow, I will indicate where librarians can offer key services to elements of your teaching of research processes.

One complicating factor in what follows is the existence of interdisciplinary courses, which present their own separate challenges. For some insight into teaching research processes within an interdisciplinary context, see O'Connor and Newby (2011). In essence, an interdisciplinary course is generally better called multidisciplinary in that various disciplines cooperate in the study of something that crosses their boundaries. This means that there will still be disciplinary thinking, but each approach to the subject matter will seek cooperation with each other approach. For now, let's consider possible options within the more traditional disciplines where most higher education instruction is done.

The humanities

Research in the humanities is distinguished, first, by the fact that it does not generally involve experimentation and, second, by its reliance on textual sources for its knowledge base and information sources. This can be baffling to those in the social sciences and sciences who wonder how we can speak of evidence and certainty in a world in which truth claims are not tested by statistically and experimentally valid results. Yet, there are methods in the humanities that offer at least a goodly measure of certainty about research results, a certainty, which like a challenge to the result of a science experiment, may be overthrown by a further presentation of evidence.

Understanding the knowledge base

The humanities pay very close attention to the distinction between primary and secondary sources, the former being seen as the most significant type of resource for advanced study. Thus, the researcher is intent on studying the primary documents themselves, analyzing them, and coming to an understanding of their meaning or significance. The researcher then produces secondary literature which, in turn, becomes a resource for the second role of the researcher – argumentation among the various interpretations of primary literature, all of them claiming to have understood that literature critically (and more accurately?). This may be an oversimplification, but it forms a good starting point for teaching research processes.

Initially, students who are seeking to be on the inside of the disciplinary research process need to experience the ways in which scholars analyze primary literature and debate with one another about it. In order to ensure that students are learning content as well as process, a good way to introduce the knowledge base is to take students directly to foundational pieces of primary literature in the discipline, and then to guide them through key secondary interpretations.

Students actually need to read the resources involved, but they will have little sense of the significance of this data unless professors do a close reading of significant passages with them, pointing out the ways in which the foundational literature of the discipline has developed through analysis, theory, counter-theory, rejoinder, and so on. The key element here is that *you can teach content by walking students through key works and helping them understand the processes at play*. The more hands-on experience students have with the literature of the discipline, under professorial guidance, the better grasp they will have of the nature of the discipline's literature.

To understand the literature of a discipline in the humanities, students also need to understand the role of peer review, the significance of scholar-to-scholar recognition of key players and key ideas (rarely done by citation counts), and the emerging roles of non-traditional publications (blogs, wikis, and so on). Overall, students need to grasp what is a valid resource for research and what is not. Inevitably, many students will not, by looking at a citation, understand the difference between a journal article and an essay in a book or even a book itself, so the teaching of distinctions in citation may well be a means to help students to make sense of the nature of the literature.

Understanding the disciplinary metanarrative

Metanarrative in the humanities is inherently rationalistic, something that burdens at least some of its proponents who live within a Postmodern worldview. The humanities are governed by the idea that human reason, guided by agreed-upon interpretive principles, can analyze the primary resources at their disposal, and come to an understanding of them. In turn, it is expected that others, using the same interpretive principles, may take varying positions, and that the scholars in the various schools of thought will use agreed-upon principles and conventions to debate with one another, with the hope of finding a resolution.

While the goal of study in the humanities was at one time discovery of the "truth," metanarrative, in these postmodern times, now seeks the less lofty goal of achieving the best explanation. Thus, there is no sense of "proof" of ideas, nor of closure of a debate, so you will rarely find all sides agreeing that they have now concluded the matter and have settled on one interpretation. Thus, whether it is a historian debating the causes of the Second Gulf War, a philosopher studying the views of Nietzsche on human beings, or an art critic seeking to understand Van Gogh's "Starry Night," the scholar in the humanities can expect steady work from the fact that few views remain unchallenged for long. The key to the metanarrative is the quest, the seeking for a better way of seeing.

For students, the literature itself can provide a good model for the nature of the discipline's quest, as long as students are introduced to the ways in which scholars interact on an interpretation. Students, as well, can be given their first assignment here. Gather examples of four or five key arguments on a significant element of the discipline's subject matter and have students analyze each argument, then declare, with reasons, why one is favored over the others. This can be accomplished as an in-class group effort or an individual take-home project. Whatever is done, the professor must then follow up the assignment with a vigorous analysis of the types of responses made by students, pointing out where method or thinking is flawed and helping students understand the sorts of questions they should have asked, as well as the ways in which they should have handled the evidence. Having done this, you have already begun introducing students to the method of the discipline, to which we now turn.

Developing skill in disciplinary method

The development of student skills in research processes is accomplished by a combination of instruction and a good deal of practice. Students in the humanities need to understand from the beginning that they will be expected to perform a lot of exercises in order to become insiders in the discipline. There may be resistance, but a creative professor can use a more process-orientated classroom to advantage in engaging students in the same sort of quest that has long fascinated their teacher.

Method is a complex combination of subject knowledge and ability to work with the conventions that built the knowledge base of the discipline from the beginning. Here, enlisting the aid of academic librarians can work wonders. Librarians can help students appreciate the importance, for example, of formulating a clear and narrowly focused goal for a research project, something that the majority of students in higher education do not seem to grasp from the assignment requirements stated by their professors.

Students learn to do research by being guided through research projects, getting both instruction and detailed feedback as they go. Having two or more research projects for students is a good start, but students need specific guidance in process at each step. This is best done by breaking such projects down into separate modules, something that is common practice these days. Each module, however, should do more than lead to a piece of content. It should be a means to teach process. If possible, students should submit each module in turn, have it critiqued, and then students who have not reached a required threshold should re-submit the module for further critique. This may appear laborious, but any skill develops only by practice, feedback and another try.

Have your students in the first module suggest *research questions* or *thesis statements* that will guide their research projects. In concert with an academic librarian, critique those research statements. What sorts of challenges can you as the professor expect to see? The most common errors are research questions or theses that are too broad, that view research as the gathering of existing information rather than the solving of a problem, that are vague or multiple in their goals, that are open-ended and thus open to multiple answers, and so on. In my student textbook on research processes (Badke, 2011b: Appendix One), I have provided numerous examples of these sorts of errors and ways to correct them. Within the humanities, lack of a clear, problem-orientated goal expressed in a single question or statement will inevitably result in a broad-based, rambling product that shows no sense of purpose. Careful attention to critiquing student research statements and having them rewrite such statements will pay off mightily in the ongoing research.

Thus, students will learn to avoid the following sorts of research questions in favor of better formulations:

Avoid: What was the importance of Nietzsche's thought?

Better: To what extent did Nietzsche's interpretation of the "Superman" accord with the national aspirations of Germany in his time?

Avoid: What can we learn from Van Gogh's painting, "Starry Night?"

Better: In light of Van Gogh's own doubts about the quality of his painting, "Starry Night," are art critics justified in labeling it a masterpiece?

Avoid: What were the events that led to the Second Gulf War?

Better: Are critics of the Second Gulf War justified in asserting that its main impetus was a desire to protect oil interests in the area?

The second module should involve an academic librarian in several sessions to help students work with databases and determine the sorts of information needed, the tools that will help find that information, the means to optimize the tools, and the skills to determine the nature of the found results. Once again, these module assignments can be critiqued, and students falling below your identified threshold can be given guided practice or an opportunity to resubmit, based on feedback. Be sure with this module that students state their research questions or theses so that the searches done and the results generated can be evaluated for relevance to the problem at hand.

The third module could be a preliminary annotated bibliography in which students would assess the quality and contribution of each of the resources found. Look for resources that are tightly focused on the research question. Warning flags are too many resources that are much broader in scope than the research question or widely diverse resources, each of which only attacks only one aspect of the research question.

Even the final project submission can be assessed for process. How well is the final research statement formulated? Does the student stay on course in addressing the research question? Are counter-arguments included and addressed or is the development one-sided? Does the student present evidence well and according to the conventions of the discipline? Is the bibliography actually used in the paper or is there too much reliance on only one or two resources? Overall, to what extent does the project look like published work in the discipline?

The social sciences

The social sciences, originating from the discipline of philosophy, have had a rough road establishing credibility within academia. Whether it be psychology, sociology, political science or some other subject area, the social sciences have struggled to be recognized as "scientific" and thus to find acceptance in academia for their findings. The challenge is compounded by the fact that the common denominator in all social sciences is the study of people. The study of people does not encourage the same sorts of conclusive findings as does, for example, a chemical reaction where ingredients and processes can be replicated indefinitely, with the same results.

Understanding the knowledge base

The social sciences are strongly theory-based. The scholar, through research and experience, develops theories of how people function as individuals and in groups. Those theories are tested through further research and seem inevitably to be challenged by counter-theories. Thus the knowledge base of the social sciences, to an even greater extent than the humanities, is characterized by flux.

The study of people is a frustrating one, due to their inherent tendency neither to be categorized easily nor to behave the same way consistently. There are inherent dissonances between what people say they believe and how they act. At times they cannot even explain their own actions, which may be altruistic or selfish depending on a multitude of possible causative factors.

Thus the social sciences are ever seeking to enhance the rigor of their research so that at least something can be said for certain, or nearly for certain (Lilienfeld, 2011). They have come a long way in this regard, finding means, for example, to be convincing about cause and effect relationships, and to be able to identify major tendencies in the ways people or groups may be expected to act within particular circumstances. Social scientists thus place a high value upon method and proper use of evidence in order to construct a knowledge base, which, though constantly evolving, they hope will be considered valid, not just among social scientists but within the larger academic community.

Students need to understand that the most highly valued information within the social sciences is the well-tested theory that can serve as a valid predictor of behavior. Peer-reviewed research is the foundation of good theory, and the challenging of theories with solid empirical evidence is a hallmark of rigor in the social sciences.

Understanding the disciplinary metanarrative

Within social scientific disciplines, the quests for explanation and the ability to predict behaviors drive all research. Humans, whether individually or in groups, are complicated beings. It is a hard task to understand how and why they function as they do within particular situations. Whether it is the bipolar individual who operates from a worldview that has unusual ideation, the motorcycle gang that justifies its actions in the midst of an aberrant subculture, the political party that works the system to its own ends, or the business that needs to improve its internal communication systems, the social sciences seek to theorize and support with evidence the processes that exist. What is more, those theories then serve as better predictors of future behavior for the same subject(s) and circumstances.

Explaining and predicting human behavior have a high value for social scientists, but so does credibility, found in research that is rigorously structured and carefully done, so that the results are accepted both within and outside of the scientific community. The disastrously inaccurate predictions of some economists over the past decade have, for example, had those economists rethinking their theories and methods in the face of a great deal of skepticism about the value of economists to society. At the same time, to do them justice, many of the past dire warnings of the best of the economists have fallen on deaf ears in society, so the problem may be more one of a failure in listeners than of faulty research. Still, this example demonstrates how important it is to social scientists to get it right and have others accept their findings. To this end, a ringing element of the metanarrative of social science is doing research that stands up to both the tests of explanation and of predictability.

To reinforce the metanarratives of the social sciences, professors should tailor their autobiographies to show their own quests for explanation and predictability. What is more, they should use examples (like the economic crisis of 2008 and following) to demonstrate the social scientific search for evidence-based theory that can foster accurate predictability.

Developing skill in disciplinary method

Research within the social sciences varies in nature from reviews of previous research to qualitative and quantitative studies. Each has its own conventions and ground rules. Foundational for information research at the student level is the often misunderstood "literature review." Students often do not grasp the point of literature reviews in general, seeing them as simply a description of previous studies on a topic, a sort of extended annotated bibliography.

Here, the simple exercise of doing close readings with students of some key literature reviews can meet both the goals of content assimilation and of helping to clarify the nature of literature review method. In essence, this is what students need to understand about literature reviews.

The goal of a literature review is to explain what has been done within a certain subject area, including the types of studies published, the key players in this field, *and then to provide a direction for what still needs to be done.* I like to think of literature reviews as narratives, starting with earlier research and coming down to the most recent. But they must never be simply a list of studies (books, articles) with a bit of commentary. Instead, they need to revolve around themes or emphases. You might indicate what people were thinking about the subject at the beginning, then how the emphasis changed. You might spell out various schools of thought that developed around the topic and explain significant examples of the studies of the major scholars supporting those schools of thought. Overall you want the reader to have a strong sense of the best work that has been done on the topic or issue. Then, near the end of the review, you need to point to something that still needs to be done. This could be a gap that remains in our knowledge, previous studies that need to be replicated with larger or different subject pools, or some flaw in the research to date that needs to be corrected. That gap, need or flaw then becomes a launching pad for further research.

Another form of literature review is an assessment of existing studies to determine whether they confirm a certain hypothesis, are complete enough to form a theory, or have some basic flaw that needs correction. This type places a fairly high-level demand upon students, but such papers can stand on their own as full research projects.

How do social science professors enhance the skills of their students in handling the literature of their disciplines? Once again, modular approaches to student assignments can work wonders. The first module needs to establish the basic research statement (question, hypothesis, etc.) so that students have a clear mental picture of the goal they are seeking. The research statement will commonly need to identify at least the gap or problem in the existing research that needs to be filled with further research. Student submissions that fail to meet the criteria for a good research statement need to be critiqued and returned for a second try and resubmission.

When it comes to the second module – identification of the literature to be reviewed and the actual acquisition of it – the role of academic librarians in assisting students is crucial unless you as their professor are fully up to date on all the nuances of databases. There is a dual challenge with researching for literature reviews. First, students must use complex databases to identify studies on their topics. Second, students must cull out of all those studies the ones that are the most essential. Librarians can help with both issues, guiding students in optimizing advanced database features, and using tools like citation counting databases (Web of Science, Google Scholar) as well as citation chaining, to determine who are the major players and what are the most significant studies. Working with a librarian from the point of student identification of research problems through the identification and location of the right studies can make the difference between students understanding the process well and simply muddling through it.

It is best, for the third assignment module, simply to have students present a bibliography, hopefully briefly annotated, of the most significant studies on the topic. Critiquing it is intended merely to make sure that the list adequately represents significant studies, that extraneous material is removed and that what is left is the core of the best research.

The fourth module will have the students build their bibliographies into literature review narratives that conclude with identification of the gaps discovered, inadequacies that need to be corrected, and so on. Or, in the case of a larger review article, the narrative may end by assessing the degree to which the case has been made for a particular theory. Whatever the goal, your assessment of student work is going to need to consider whether the narrative is coherent, all relevant schools of thought are represented, and if the analysis that concludes the literature review is rigorous and valid. Librarians, well used to the process of literature reviews, will be helpful in your assessment of this module as well.

Method in the social sciences is not something that can be taught in a single assignment. If your class is structured to study literature reviews, the discourse patterns of various types of research, and the assessment of research, you will help students begin to get it. What they are "getting" is a grasp of the way things are done in your discipline. Along the way, they need a lot of practice in doing their own literature reviews and hopefully in participating in human research, if your research ethics people will allow that. A constant focus on process can go far toward meeting both the content needs (as they assess the literature with a view to understanding both content and method) and the needs of research skill development.

The sciences

The sciences pride themselves on asserting constantly that many findings are tentative, that the assured results of one generation could be debunked by experiments done in the next. The bedrock of the sciences, except for their most radical proponents, is the scientific method. Most everything done in science is tested by this method, and it generally, though not always, goes unchallenged. In fact, the greatest travesties in the scientific world are to abuse the method by using it unskillfully, fudging results, or making conclusions beyond what the results can reasonably demonstrate. Thus, no development of student research processes ability in the sciences can ignore the foundation of scientific method.

Understanding the knowledge base

The knowledge base of the sciences has grown incrementally through structured observation, experiments and other types of studies that use the scientific method. This growth has not been steady, however, in that the findings of the past may well be refuted by research in the present or future, thus making scientific knowledge development less a steady accumulation than a set of fits and starts that add knowledge over time while occasionally removing past conclusions that are no longer accepted. In general, for knowledge to be recognized as such in the scientific knowledge base, it needs either to have behind it multiple replicated experiments or observations, or it needs to be based on a theory which explains phenomena better than does any other theory.

It is thus not easy to add to scientific knowledge. Rigorous patterns of peer review are there to ensure that quack science does not creep into the knowledge base, though peer review is not in itself foolproof. Overall, scientists are quite tough-minded about their knowledge, testing and retesting their findings and remaining skeptical of anything that cannot be supported by a strong theory or replicated experiment. For example, "cold fusion" is a phenomenon that has never been properly supported by research and thus has been generally refuted by the scientific community (Feder, 2005).

While the knowledge base is characterized by peer-reviewed journal articles, and, to a lesser extent, books that summarize the research and establish theories, increasingly scientists are discussing their work through Web 2.0 tools like wikis and social networks. Thus you may well find a pre-publication, pre-review paper on the Internet, where the authors are seeking evaluation from fellow scientists prior to going through a more rigorous peer review process. Such studies, as well as the multitude of quasi-scientific publications available through search engines, are complicating the previous notion of a pristine knowledge base.

Whatever scientists tell their students about the scientific knowledge base, they must reckon both with the rigor of traditional approaches to publication and with the newer forces that are innovative but tend to muddy the waters in which university students are immersed.

Understanding the disciplinary metanarrative

Scientific research is governed by a sense of quest that stresses discovery and explanation. With an agreed-upon scientific method, the metanarrative of the sciences is built on feeding the quest with data that has been rigorously obtained and can be replicated. Data eventually leads to theory (larger explanations) and very occasionally to laws (the most assured results of research).

Scientists are for the most part sold on the process that leads to their data and to theories and laws, so much so that any misuse of the scientific method is greeted with resounding condemnation. To say that the method of science has godlike status is scarcely an exaggeration. To be sure "scientific method" has been challenged on the grounds that the concept is too diverse in its interpretations to be constituted as a method (see, for example, Bouffard, 2001, and the rejoinder by Shephard, 2001), yet there is a time-honored traditional understanding of what we mean by science that has withstood all attempts to debunk or fragment it.

Those who teach research in the sciences must begin with philosophy of science, which both debunks false ideas about science (such as the possibility of proof) and frames scientific method as the way science must be done if it wants to continue to have respectability in academia and beyond. Science professors, as well, need to make strong use of autobiography to reveal the interests that led them into the field, the struggles they faced, the current work they are doing, and so on. We want students to enter our world with enthusiasm and skill. They will only do that if they catch the passion of those already in that world.

Developing skill in disciplinary method

While some students may well, in more senior years or at graduate level, be doing a few significant experiments of their own, the teaching of research processes will likely deal with two main areas – literature reviews and replication of earlier experiments. I will leave the latter to the science professors who generally already have sophisticated training in place. Literature reviews are another story. While many of the same sorts of challenges, procedures and teaching methods seen in social sciences can be followed in the sciences, there tends in the sciences to be less scope for varied interpretation of results or for schools of thought to develop, because processes in the physical world tend to be more precise than in the world of human beings. Still, the literature review in the sciences, like the social sciences, is a narrative intended to lead to a perceived gap that justifies yet one more experiment or study.

Science professors, like those in the social sciences, need to recognize that literature reviews are not intuitively simple but are mystifying and confusing to the average student. Close reading of good reviews can be a great way to teach method while helping students assimilate content. And critique of student-created literature reviews, with a request for revised versions when they are not done to expectation, will help students develop skill in structuring and writing review projects.

The sciences demand a lot of content learning, but a good amount of the content can be covered by going through the significant literature with students, helping them to understand method along with content. Have students evaluate experimental papers, identifying the various parts, summarizing them and determining the extent to which the experiments met the goals of the original hypotheses. Keep their minds on method even as you teach content, so that the metanarrative of the sciences – discovery by the scientific method – may become ingrained.

Databases devoted to scientific literature can be more complex than those in the social sciences and humanities. Many of these tools rely on the precision of scientific language and thus do not provide subject headings. Here, academic librarians can help students to learn how to narrow often enormous result sets to the most important studies, adding defining terminology and enlisting the aid of citation counts and citation chaining. Since these librarians well understand the requirements of literature reviews, they offer more than mere "library instruction" but can actually help students further the goals of their literature reviews.

It is helpful to modularize student projects, evaluate the various parts for the ability that students show in "doing" the discipline, provide clear feedback, and call for revised versions of work that is not at the required level. Once again, this is not a one-off procedure but something that needs to be practiced through many courses and, indeed, right through programs. Skills will develop, but they require both time and practice.

Professional programs

Professional programs such as business, education, medicine, law, and so on, share the common characteristic of wedding theory and praxis with a view to improving the latter. Ultimately, it is the quality of praxis that determines the value of the professional program. Research in this field is diverse but we can find commonalities. A demographic study intended to determine the potential success of a business venture may be akin to what a historian does when she analyzes primary sources. An evidence-based medical study may well be identical in method to scientific research. What professional programs have in common is their zeal to improve the quality of application of research to real-life situations.

Understanding the knowledge base

The knowledge base in professional programs is in constant flux, factors of the fact that the human situations in which professionals do their practice are constantly changing and that any research intended primarily to improve praxis is bound to find new ways of doing things. Thus the business person, nurse, or member of the clergy of thirty years ago operated under different parameters than do corresponding practitioners today.

The professional knowledge base, as well, is shaped as much by the experience of its practitioners as it is by more "objective" research procedures. This works two ways: Experience tells practitioners what works and what doesn't, and experience can also be an impetus to research that seeks newer and better ways to accomplish tasks that have changed over time.

"Method" for research in professional programs is characterized by a tendency to the eclectic, so much so that we must speak of "methods" rather than method. Helping students, therefore, to understand the nature of the knowledge base for the professions within our changing professional climates is a daunting task. What are the best sources for knowledge within our discipline? Can we speak of "knowledge" when what we know is constantly shifting? What sources do we trust, and why? These and other foundational questions must be addressed so that students understand how we can say that we know what we know. They must also grasp that the professions hold their "knowledge" with rather open hands, recognizing that the current version of reality may be overthrown in whole or part at any time.

Understanding the disciplinary metanarrative

For the professions, well-informed, up-to-date, and effective practice is of paramount importance. All professions share a measure of what could be called "professional pride," which is based on a mixture of competency, service and ethics. Many are characterized by colleges or boards that regulate qualifications and practices of practitioners, thus elevating the profession as a whole. The research quest in professional programs is set upon constantly finding new ways to better accomplish the professional task.

The metanarratives of professions all go something like this: "I am a _____ who is intent on bringing the best knowledge and practices together to the accomplishment of the tasks of my profession. More efficient, effective, helpful, and ethical service to my clientele is my central motivation."

Professional programs are better at communicating their metanarrative than most other university departments, most likely because the professions are the most closely aligned with the goals of actual practice of the discipline. You do not study to be a doctor, nurse, educator, lawyer or business person without being constantly reminded that, at the end of the education process, you will need to be certified and to carry out your profession with real people. Thus the values of better praxis, informed by sound research data, are part and parcel of most everything that students in the professions are learning.

Developing skill in disciplinary method

We should likely be discussing disciplinary "methods" rather than "method," because they are so diverse, not just among the various professional disciplines but even within them. That said, the methodologies of the professions are much more front and center in university programs than, say, in the humanities. Research method, after all, is intended to inform praxis and thus must be central to all professional study.

I have discovered, and the research literature (see Chapter 2 in this volume) has confirmed, however, that students in professional programs are no more rigorously trained in research processes than are students in other professions. What seems to be happening is that, while students in professional study are given numerous research assignments, they are not receiving the guidance they need to carry out those assignments.

I recall interacting with a Master of Business Administration student tasked with researching a complex problem. She was using only Google Scholar, which did not have the ability to focus her search to find the information she needed. When I suggested that she use her institution's subscription to EBSCO's *Business Source Complete*, she confessed that she didn't know what that was. This from a graduate student. Sending her out to do research without the requisite background had proven to be a recipe for frustration.

Academic librarians with knowledge in professions can be extremely useful in helping you to identify the education needs of your students in professional programs. Whether that is by helping students to clarify research goals and use the multitude of business databases to advantage, or advancing the cause of evidence-based medicine in a nursing program, academic librarians are highly skilled at putting a finger on the gaps that need to be filled before research assignments in your program actually serve to advance student skills.

For the professions, the problem is not that students have little opportunity to do research but that there is a lack of guidance in research processes that can make all that research practice profitable.

Conclusion

This chapter has provided a sketch of what research processes instruction might look like in various disciplinary settings. Actual curricula will flesh out these ideas dramatically. The one thing we want to avoid, however, is to give the impression that a few tips, applied in a limited number of selected teaching situations, is going to create skilled student researchers. Rather, these examples are intended to foster a different way of thinking in which process takes center stage with content, and the teaching of research processes becomes a significant part of the foundation of instruction. Process thinking about the knowledge base, metanarrative and method of the discipline forms the basis for instruction that helps students actually to enter the world of the discipline rather than merely being outside observers of it. To enable students to become skilled researchers demands that they receive consistent, long-term instruction and guided practice in the elements of research processes.

Clearly, what we now need to consider is how such efforts would look across a university system or even one of its departments. To that consideration we now turn.

8

Research processes transforming education

Abstract: In order to develop the teaching of research processes within the university, a grassroots approach is preferable. Individual professors implement research processes instruction by using such elements as autobiography, information-based instruction, guided modular assignments, involvement of students in the professor's own research, and options made available by new information technologies. The grassroots approach widens with departmental involvement that succeeds only if logical, emotional and situational barriers are overcome. Finally, university-wide initiatives can be started through a process of discussion among professors and departments. Such initiatives need to develop a campus-wide educational philosophy, create research and writing courses in each discipline, and put forward a comprehensive plan to meet specific research processes instruction goals through the curriculum.

Key words: autobiography, comprehensive plan, grassroots approach, information technologies, information-based instruction, modular assignments.

Up to this point, we have identified a problem and provided some suggestions for a solution. The following chapter will take a broader look at the nature of a higher educational venture that makes research processes fundamental to education. We are seeking a new vision of education in which the handling of information with skill and understanding is the basis of all instruction and all student work.

The educational task of the professor

If you are a professor, you may be asking yourself how you could possibly implement a new vision for education in a setting in which you are tasked with delivering subject matter to students, covering a curriculum, and having students achieve acceptable grades on examinations or other assessment measures. To step out of the comfort zone of doing what we have been doing is indeed a challenge.

Let me suggest, however, that it is possible to test the waters, implementing research processes-based initiatives one at a time. Here are some key elements that can be included fairly easily and can go a long way toward achieving your traditional educational goals.

The power of autobiography

Most students are interested in who their professors are, if only to determine how difficult it will be to achieve a good grade with a particular teacher. To begin your courses with some measure of autobiography (while seeking to ensure that the same students do not hear the same story too often) will accomplish several purposes:

- It will humanize you. Believe it or not, many students see their professors as another species that is unaccountably enthusiastic about the incomprehensible and distinctly lacking a real life outside of the classroom. Humanization is a positive good in that it opens the possibility and attractiveness of student entry into the professor's discipline. When we are aloof and superior, we send the message that we intend to tell students about our disciplines but never to let them enter. This, obviously, disengages them.

- It will enable you to speak more easily about the metanarrative of your discipline, about the beliefs, values and passions that drive practitioners. For students to "get" the metanarrative is crucial, because it is the metanarrative that defines the discipline, every bit as much as its method.

- It will open the possibility that your students could follow your own path into the discipline. You were not always part of your discipline's in-crowd. Helping students understand how you got there (including your joys, sorrows, victories and failures along the way) can offer hope that at least some of your students will do the same.

- Autobiography still teaches content if it includes your understanding of how the discipline works, what its main passions are, and how you have been influenced by its main proponents. You have essentially, with autobiography, an open door to better reception of content.

Information-based instruction

There is a profound difference between teaching *about* the discipline and teaching through the literature of the discipline. Teaching through the literature means that students get to study the actual materials that form the basis of research processes. In a history course, for example, you could teach the events surrounding the beginning of the First World War by going over with students the actual documents issued by various parties (as found, for example, at *http://www. firstworldwar.com/source/1914.htm*). Your analysis would include not merely content but the method used in determining the beliefs, prejudices, propaganda, and so on that lie behind the documents. If historical study requires the interpretation of primary sources, you can demonstrate both the metanarrative of the study of European history and the methods used to *do* that discipline.

For the social sciences and sciences, close reading of key literature reviews can foster both content and an understanding of research processes. Such close reading helps students to understand the way scholars express their approach to the discipline, the sorts of discourse and debate that work to advance the topic at hand, and the very structure and purpose of a good review. You can trace the development of theories, advancement of scientific knowledge through experimentation, and so on, simply relying on the literature itself to point the way.

In all disciplines, while textbooks can be helpful, and the best of them incorporate some direct use of the literature of the discipline, they tend to be secondary overall, teaching about the discipline rather than inviting students to work within it. Studying a discipline's direct literature can help students learn the nature of the information base they are to work with, the metanarratives that guide each discipline, the methods used, and the views of the major scholars who define the state of the art. A process of using more primary materials and fewer secondary ones will not necessarily disrupt the traditional educational goals if done carefully, but it will help students to become research process insiders much more quickly than if they are simply told *about* the subject matter from the distance of secondary study.

Guided, modular assignments

We have seen that many students struggle with understanding the expectations of their professors, no matter how carefully those professors try to explain what they require. A corrective to this problem, and a means to develop student researchers in an intentional way, is to assign research projects which both approximate real research in the discipline and offer opportunity for professorial feedback and resubmission of revised work.

Two barriers to this approach to assignments are immediately apparent. First, students who must resubmit work will balk at the extra effort required. This problem can be overcome by stating the resubmission requirement from the outset or possibly even limiting the number of research projects in order to allow for resubmission to be done within normal student workloads. Second, this approach is labor-intensive for the professor, who not only has several assignment modules to grade rather than just one, but who will need to be more expansive in assessment comments and will need to similarly grade resubmissions. I am not sure I have a good answer to this except to ask: Is the professor's task to disseminate information or foster student learning? If the latter, we are going to have to get used to providing much more feedback on student work so that students not only understand requirements clearly but are enabled to do the work of disciplinarians, producing results that stand up to the rigor demanded by each discipline.

Modules – such as development of a research question or thesis/hypothesis, determination of the information required, acquisition of relevant literature, evaluation of that literature for relevance and quality, and writing of the final project – will not succeed in enhancing research processes unless both instructions and grading foster the work of developing student researchers. Thus instruction on creating research questions or theses/hypotheses should include good examples or at least helpful guidelines. Feedback should point out reasons for inadequacies (research statements are too open-ended, vague, using information as a goal rather than a tool, not capable of being addressed with evidence, etc.) and reasons why a good research statement works (states a clearly focused research problem that demands rigorous analysis of data in order to address the issue, etc.). With every module you must give as much attention to the student's method and information-handling ability as you do to the content on the page.

Once again, though possibly self-serving on my part, may I suggest strongly that academic librarians can be of tremendous help, both in providing consultation on the design of assignment modules and in suggesting ways to assess student work. Librarians should also be brought into the classroom to help students understand the nature of the literature in the discipline and the expert use of today's complex information databases. More on this shortly.

Involving students in your own research

While the actual direct involvement of students in their professors' research is limited by logistics (you can only take on so many helpers) and generally confined to graduate study, introducing students to your own work in process is a significant way to help them see the discipline in action. Whether you have them summarize some of your publications, or critique them (I've done the latter and found it painful but constructive), engaging students in this way invites them in more definitely than do many other efforts.

Small beginnings, larger ends

Once you are able to demonstrate to yourself and hopefully to your superiors that such research-based initiatives both meet traditional educational goals and engage students more deeply, you can hopefully develop further the means to teach research processes even as you are teaching content. Here are some ideas:

- Wikipedia encourages the creation and editing of articles as university course assignments (*http://en.wikipedia.org/wiki/Wikipedia:School_and_university_projects*). With clear advice and guidelines available, students can produce or revise Wikipedia articles under the guidance of a professor. Tracking the external edits of created articles can provide students with sound (and perhaps sobering) feedback on the principles and practices expected of those researching within the discipline.

- There are numerous Web 2.0 options for the development of research projects – wikis, threaded discussions, blogs with feedback, incorporation of videos and animations, and so on – which can enable students to do "works in process," thus building their skills as individuals or within groups. The key is to keep them researching, writing and continuously receiving feedback, followed by resubmission. We are often so keen on viewing the final product that we miss opportunities to use process to refine student skills. Web 2.0 is filled with process tools to do the latter. For more on use of Web 2.0 in teaching research processes, see Hicks and Graber (2010).

- Begin thinking through all the courses you teach. Is it possible for you to establish research processes development goals for each course so that, as much as it is in your hands, there is a progression of experiences from basic, initial levels to more sophisticated opportunities as students move from lower to upper years? With such a plan in place, and assessment data to show that students are indeed developing as researchers, you will be in a strong position to justify placing research processes development at the foundation of your teaching. You will also have data to help persuade your colleagues to attempt the same in their courses.

- Assess your instruction in research processes. Beyond your own grading of student assignments, there are numerous research pretests and post-tests available (do an Internet search on <information literacy pretest>) as well as professional tests of research ability such as Project Sails (*https://www.projectsails.org/*), iSkills (*http://www.ets.org/iskills/about*), and Information Literacy Test (*http://www.madisonassessment.com/assessment-testing/information-literacy-test/*). RAILS (Rubric Assessment of Information Literacy Skills) provides numerous rubrics for all aspects of research processes (*http://www.railsontrack.info/*). Your assessment will provide data that enables you to speak with authority about the effectiveness of your work in developing student researchers. For more on assessment techniques in research processes instruction, see Oakleaf (2009) and Oakleaf and Kaske (2009).

Departmental planning for teaching research processes

A single lonely professor actively teaching research processes can become a pathetic object of amusement and/or scorn if there is no departmental support. Questions arise as to whether or not content is being covered, and the professor may be told that research skills cannot be taught but must be learned by students doing research on their own. Thus, enlisting departmental support is crucial to furthering the teaching of research processes in the institution.

There are significant barriers, however, the predominant one being that most academics do not see that there is a problem to be solved. Students are poor researchers, to be sure, but we already have the best that we can hope for. In general, there are few models for advancing student research skills beyond giving more assignments and trying to motivate our students to take them seriously.

How does a professor, charged up by a new experience of actually teaching research processes as a foundational element of courses, overcome departmental barriers to expanding such instruction? Here, an extremely helpful book – *Switch: How to Change Things When Change Is Hard* (Heath and Heath, 2010) – may provide a solution. The authors argue that difficult change must address the logical, emotional and situational factors that stand in the way.

The logical barrier is the one with which we are most familiar. People are not convinced that research processes can be taught or should be given priority. This barrier is overcome by providing a logically convincing argument. You need a persuasive way to explain to departmental members the specific steps you took (autobiography, a focus on the nature of information sources and metanarrative of the discipline, staged and guided research assignments, and so on) and show evidence that you are meeting your goals (which are generally also departmental goals) – creating competent researchers who can state a research problem, determine information sources needed to address it, find those sources, evaluate them and apply them to the problem at hand.

The emotional aspect of change focuses on what Heath and Heath call "finding the feeling." In the case of research processes, "the feeling" is that lecture methods are not working as well as we had hoped and that students are disengaged, showing little interest in involving themselves deeply with the discipline, nor having any real ability to do so. Their use of information and their ability to do significant research are lacking, so much so that many professors have "dumbed down" their requirements. We wanted critical thinkers and genuine interest in the subject matter, but we so often get what looks like apathy and indifference. Amazingly, students, who are paying for their education (or their parents are), demonstrate a profound disinterest in actually being educated. Many of them see themselves as simply paying for a diploma.

This generates a strong emotional sense of dread that we, as educators, are not succeeding. Perceived failure is a great motivator to seeking new ways to do things, but ongoing failure, according to Heath and Heath, creates a general sense of exhaustion, a belief that there is nothing we can do to change things or that the effort we would have to make to bring about significant change is just too much.

To overcome this inertia, we need to break the change needed down into smaller components. We could, for example, tell our fellow departmental members about the power of autobiography to get students interested in our subject matter. We could show how staging an assignment is something many are already doing but that, if we made each stage an opportunity to guide students in proper research procedure, we would go a long way toward teaching research processes.

A large factor in emotional buy-in to change is creating a community of like-minded people. Establishing such a community is furthered by your demonstrated success. If you as a professor show your colleagues that your students are now beginning to use their critical faculties more, are actually showing interest in the discipline, and are becoming a joy to teach, you will have strong buy-in. Aren't these exactly the sorts of things all of us as educators are looking for? If there is a way to achieve such goals, we're in.

Yet there are still situational challenges. We've never done this before. It's a lot of work to change our teaching methods. How do we know it will work? Will we be able to prove to our colleagues and administrators that we are still pursuing good education? Are there any intrinsic or extrinsic rewards for the effort we will need to make? Heath and Heath suggest that, in the face of situational challenges, we need to change the environment, create habits and "rally the herd."

In the case of departmental adoption of a program of teaching research processes, may I suggest that most departments have the tools already in hand to alter the environment. These tools are the existing vision, mission and goals that define the departmental ethos. In these documents lie the best aspirations of the stakeholders – both academic administrators and faculty. To have a department go honestly over these aspiration documents and identify where goals are not being met is a significant first start. If we are not producing critical thinkers who are able to articulate the principles of the discipline and work intelligently within it, we are not producing skilled student researchers either.

Once it is recognized that goals are not being met, the work of any professor actually teaching research processes in the department is going to become a model for broader departmental change. What if departmental members were to get together and produce a further document, not a statement of goals, but an action plan to meet them, using the principles and methods of research processes instruction? Such a shared document, with concrete, achievable steps pointing the way forward, could then provide the "permission" to change. If we as a department can decide together to take active steps in all of our courses to alter our approach, then we are well down the road to teaching research processes department-wide. Such steps begin to create the habit of considering processes instruction as being every bit as integral to the foundation of education as the teaching of content (process actually often being used as a tool to teach content). And such habits, practiced together, encourage the whole "herd" of departmental personnel to further the cause.

Once again, a strong ally in furthering broader teaching of research processes will be the academic librarian. Why? Because academic librarians see the student side of the problem. They encounter, on a daily basis, all of the inadequacies of student understanding and ability. Academic librarians know the truth, while faculty members are often shielded from it by student reticence to reveal their personal research flaws to their teachers. Those flaws come out directly and often in student reference encounters with librarians. These same librarians have had decades of experience with teaching research processes, and their published literature on the topic is significant. Use them as advocates for departmental transition to foundational research processes instruction. They will be highly supportive and immensely helpful.

Yet there is the nagging question: Why should departments and their professors make the change? Higher education has weathered challenges since the Renaissance and earlier, yet we still have professors, lectures and students. Why not perpetuate what works? The answers vary from considering the profound economic and administrative changes that are attacking the tenure system (Berrett, 2011) to being alarmed by new studies that are showing that our undergraduate students do not appear to be learning anything near as much as we think they are (Arum and Roksa, 2011). But the real problem we are facing is that the technology of information has made information itself a cheap commodity while at the same time attacking, and perhaps defeating, the power of informational expertise that once came from safeguards like peer review (Badke, 2009b). Our students don't need us if all we are going to do is disseminate information. What they actually require is our expertise, something we can only prove to them if we make the teaching of research processes foundational to instruction.

Our students are terrible information handlers both conceptually and operationally. They don't even have nearly the technological ability we credit them for (Stone and Madigan, 2007). These gaps are large contributors to their increased disconnection from what we are teaching them. We have an opportunity to bring them in by guiding them to become skilled student researchers, thus making them growing disciplinarians and meeting all of our motherhood goals of critical thinking and skilled discourse within the subject matter. The question is not, why should we change? but what sort of death wish are we promoting by refusing to change?

University planning for teaching research processes

If you have been following the progression of this chapter, you will see that I have been arguing for a grassroots approach that begins with individual professors who in turn evangelize their departments, leading to a broader university-wide transition. As departments begin to show success in teaching research processes, the Heath and Heath (2010) methods for effecting change can enable departments to evangelize their universities.

It is not beyond the realm of possibility to create a research processes teaching university. Let me suggest some stages.

First, it is vitally important that universities begin establishing philosophies of instruction that actually carry weight. The grassroots approach I've suggested may well be a better path to developing such policies through departmental collaboration rather than top-down fiat. A philosophy of instruction will need to acknowledge that today's educational environment is increasingly resistant to mere information dissemination. It must, as well, admit that we have an information age without a plan to enable its inhabitants to handle information effectively. Finally, it must put research processes instruction into the foundation of all educational efforts, mandating an approach to education that intentionally makes students into disciplinarians.

The second stage is to establish research and writing courses in every major. Such courses have shown themselves well able to carry the initial development of research processes thinking in students. It might be objected that such courses may be needed in the humanities, which are writing-intensive, but not in the social sciences or sciences. I would counter-argue that the social sciences and sciences need such courses precisely because there are so few other opportunities in these disciplines to teach students how to work with information and do informational research. Even the physical sciences call for information research (literature reviews) and writing.

The third stage is to ensure that every department has a comprehensive plan to integrate the teaching of research processes into the curriculum. Here, all parties must recognize that we are not considering short-term, remedial instruction, but a comprehensive approach to a problem that is akin to teaching someone fluency in a new language. Courses must be targeted and specific strategies developed to enable students to meet specific goals (e.g. able to formulate an acceptable research problem, able to maximize advanced features in a journal database, able to distinguish types of research literature, able to evaluate found resources for quality and relevance, and so on).

What about the traditional resistance of faculty members to direction from administrators? That, indeed, can be a problem if the development of research processes instruction policies and procedures is done from above. I am advocating, however, that this whole endeavor begin with classroom professors and migrate upward. If, ultimately, some professors or departments need to be persuaded from above, the arguments of this book should serve as grist. Adopting such principles as those suggested by Heath and Heath (2010) can facilitate changes of heart and practice among those who favor traditional approaches to education.

Ultimately, we are seeking universities that believe in the power of making the teaching of research processes foundational to education. In an information age, there are multiple ways to acquire the content we teach, but most students lack the process abilities to handle the information that defines their lives. Foundational teaching of research processes is the most relevant thing we can do.

If done well, we will have much more engaged students who see themselves operating *within* the discipline rather than looking at it through the filter of their professors. And we will be accomplishing what surely must be a basic requirement for citizens in the information age – the ability to harness information skillfully to address the issues and challenges of our time. We are not expecting that all of our students will become researchers at the doctoral level, simply that they become informationally adept in whatever setting they find themselves.

9

Resourcing the enterprise

Abstract: We must address the question of resourcing such a change in educational emphasis. In this case it is best first to recognize that dedication of resources to any enterprise is a matter of establishing priorities. Here the challenge is to overcome the ongoing lack of appreciation that student inability to handle information well is a pressing problem. We need to realign the tasks of academic librarians, who have been at the forefront of advocating the teaching of research processes. Their roles as consultants and team teachers must be enhanced. Further, a grassroots approach, supported by professorial autobiography, evidence-based results, a clear statement of vision and the seeking of commitments from departments and universities, is the path forward. There must, as well, be buy-in at the top in order to legitimize the teaching of research processes and facilitate both its initiation and sustainability. We already have the financial and personnel resources needed. We now need to devote them to the task.

Key words: academic administrators, academic librarians, autobiography, evidence-based, grassroots approach, resources, sustainability.

There have been a multitude of educational theories and "solutions" over the years that have died almost as soon as they were uttered. Higher education is slow to change and is generally resistant to programmatic new initiatives. This is understandable, given the investment in time and money required simply to maintain even regular programming in universities and colleges. "If it ain't broke (and many would deny it is, despite overwhelming evidence that academia is in trouble), why fix it?"

Added to the lack of desire to make the enormous effort to change, higher education is beset by traditions that once preserved it and are now increasingly simply presenting barriers to sustainability. We need only think of the past success of the lecture (making it thus a best practice), the restrictions of peer review (a good idea but needing re-evaluation) and, dare I say it, the laws of tenure that work against listening to innovators. Newer voices, especially those that speak energetically in favor of dramatic change, sound like dogs nipping at the heels of an already challenged system. Academia asks in turn, "How do we know your new idea will work? Who is going to do it and with what motivation? How are we going to resource it?"

Let me make a few suggestions.

The question of priorities

In the midst of the economic downturns of the past numbers of years, there have been many questions about how societies and families will survive. Draconian measures have often been required to balance budgets or at least limit deficits. One truth that such activity has taught us is that we fund our priorities and cut everything that is not deemed essential. While it is instructive to look at how budgets reflect priorities (eliminating school librarians but buying fighter jets), economic downturns bring to light the reality that we can resource anything we are determined to resource. It's all a matter of what is deemed to be the highest priority.

When a system comes under sufficient pressure, there is an initial search for a simple solution to solve the problem. In higher education we have had the "give them technology" movement that assumed that providing students with the right technological tools would transform them into learners. Technology by itself, however, as is becoming obvious to most learners, offers little unless students can optimize its use. They cannot do this without significant education. We have tried making students the sole authors of their own forms of active learning, to the extent of letting them set their own curricula and learning methods. This was less than successful because students need guidance from disciplinary experts.

At times, as I consider academia today, I am frustrated. The world is changing at warp speed, information technology is taking over in every aspect of our lives, and we seem helpless to make the changes needed to turn higher education into the relevant enterprise it needs to be (Badke, 2009b). We spend money on initiatives that don't work, and we miss the point that the information age is about information – how we handle it effectively to solve problems and advance knowledge. It's a process problem, and we are missing the boat.

Case in point: Head and Eisenberg (2011) published a newspaper story in which they summarized years of research with thousands of college students, the majority of whom had overwhelming difficulty starting research projects, determining what was expected of them, dealing with the abundance of information tools and content available, and managing their resources in order to write projects and make conclusions. The pointed out that inadequate information literacy is a significant problem for both students and society. These researchers have done many studies on many campuses with many students, and one would think that their results would be virtually unassailable.

Yet, the responses to this article from readers revealed an enormous gap in understanding of and empathy with their findings. Comments included calls to return to the study of the great books, to turn off the technology, to stop griping about professors, to stop believing that searching for information is difficult when it is not, and to recognize that students simply need to apply themselves more. Not one comment in the first ten showed even a remote understanding of the problem.

I made the eleventh comment as follows:

> I wasn't going to weigh in, really, but I am so frustrated that I feel I must. As an academic reference librarian with 25 years experience working with undergraduate and graduate students, and as someone who has followed Head and Eisenberg's work for several years, I have to say this: It is time for all of us to pay attention. Our students, the majority of our students, have only a dim understanding of the information base they must work with in their studies. They are dealing with an insurmountable variety of information sources, complex search tools, and a lack of understanding of the research processes demanded of them. I call this the biggest blind spot in higher education, and I see that blind spot every day in otherwise bright and well-motivated students who simply do not know how to handle the information they are called upon to deal with. Their professors may "get" information, but their students don't. Let's start paying attention. Head and Eisenberg are doing good research that confirms what any experienced academic librarian sees every day. We are failing our students. They are motivated, but we are not educating them in the information and research processes they need to understand.

Resourcing the teaching of research processes is going to take, first, a recognition of priorities. Neglect of such teaching has come from a lack of recognition that there is a problem. My conclusion, based on many research studies and my own years of experience, is that the problem is both significant and pressing. If we come to believe the same, we will readjust our priorities to make the teaching of research processes fundamental to education, on a par with the teaching of content. So, what resources are required? Surprisingly, most needed resources may already be in place, though they have not been prioritized.

Realigning academic librarians

The heroes and heroines of the teaching of research processes over the past few decades have surely been the academic librarians. They were among the first to see the problem because they are the most likely educational practitioners to encounter students struggling to perform research tasks that they neither understand nor have the skills to complete. Thus librarians took the initiative to offer their services in short-term instruction and, when allowed, credit courses in research processes. They supplemented their teaching with their own research and writing, resulting in a significant information literacy literature base that, sadly, is confined to library publications, an overblown example of preaching to the converted.

Academic librarians are spread very thinly. Many do dozens of one-shot sessions in a variety of classes. Those who teach modules or full courses in research processes may well do this as overload while maintaining roles as reference librarians. If we were to have them take on all of the sorts of work actually required to produce skilled student researchers, we would need to multiply their numbers, something that no university administer would begin to contemplate.

I would like to suggest that many of the real talents of academic librarians are not being optimized. When one's time is occupied doing remedial library instruction at the rate of one hour per student per university program, there is little opportunity to enlist librarians' more advanced knowledge and skills. Academic librarians are research processes experts. While they may lack all the disciplinary expertise of a specialized professor, they know how information works, and they spend much of their time concentrating on the development of process skills in students.

If we want to resource the teaching of research processes, we are going to need to reconfigure the roles of academic librarians, not so that they become the sole research processes instructors but so that they can spend much more time consulting with teaching faculty:

- *Substitute online tools for the one-shot.* We have a large number of tools available to introduce students to today's libraries and databases. Many of these can be used by students on their own, with testing to ensure that they are learning what they need to (Badke, 2009c). Academic librarians can thus be freed to use their real talents.

- *Enhance the consulting role of librarians.* Academic librarians are excellent consultants. They are collaborative and generally do not have large egos. In every venue where faculty plan to teach or are actually teaching research processes, academic librarians will likely be able to offer more guidance and critique than any other academics on your campus. They can analyze research assignments to determine what students will and will not understand, they can help develop plans for teaching research processes effectively in the classroom, they can advise on departmental initiatives to establish research processes instruction programs, and they can provide very helpful input for the development of institution-wide principles and practices that lead to the comprehensive teaching of research processes.

- *Embed your librarians.* Many institutions are now "embedding" librarians, the term having come from Middle East wars in which reporters travel with the troops, experiencing what they do. An embedded librarian can serve as both advisor and co-instructor within a department, making the teaching of research processes the intentional practice that it needs to be. The embedded librarian is able to use his/her abilities to much greater advantage than is possible in a multitude of introductory library instruction sessions.

- *Give librarians their due.* Academia must recognize academic librarians as highly able members of the academic team. They are not minor clerks but research process experts. Wherever they can have a place in the development of methods to meet the information literacy gap, employ their services.

Taking a grassroots approach

We have argued that the creation of a research processes emphasis in a college or university works best when individual professors catch the vision, try it out, and see its success. This does not require a lot of special resourcing, beyond having academic librarians become more deeply engaged in helping develop research processes instruction. The real genius of a grassroots approach is that those most involved in producing skilled student researchers catch the vision first and thus are motivated to enlist the support of their departments and institutions.

Resourcing the enterprise from the grassroots up tends to be much less costly in personnel and finances than does top-down implementation. Administrators often believe that the only way to establish a program is to throw money and people at the problem. Not only is this needlessly costly in additional resources, but it is expensive in the level of resentment it can produce in those who are not yet convinced of its importance. If faculty at the level of teaching can show that such efforts can be resourced without extensive funding and additional personnel, the result will be much more effective and efficient.

Getting others onside is, of course, the challenge. We have seen the approaches advocated by Heath and Heath (2010) for effecting change when change is difficult. To these, may I add the following:

- *Use the power of autobiography.* Those who are convinced of the value of teaching research processes within the foundations of their courses have a story to tell. How did you first discover the idea? What were your initial barriers and misgivings? What convinced you to try it out? How did you implement your plan? What were the initial responses of students and their later views of what you had done? What challenges did you experience? Why are you convinced that you followed the right path? Why should others emulate your activities?

- *Make it evidence-based.* Use pretests and post-tests to measure the degree of involvement with your subject matter found in students who are learning to be researchers. Get permission to post online some of your students' projects that reveal their growing skills. Never base your "pitch" merely on autobiography, as important as that is. Follow up with data that shows it works.

- *Express a vision.* Avoid simply saying that everyone should do what you are doing. Instead, tap into the deepest aspirations of your colleagues. They want to teach classes full of highly engaged students who are using critical thinking, disciplinary expertise, and the best resources they can find to produce competent research projects. Successful teaching of research processes can produce just such an outcome. Focus on the vision.

- *Call for decisive action at the department and university level.* No salesperson who avoids bringing the client to a point of decision will survive long in business. If you, as a professor, are convinced that we must begin putting the teaching of research processes at the foundation of education, then you have an opportunity to become the engineer of decisions that will bring it into being. Simply to make a pitch and get the response that we should do something about this sometime is to perpetuate what we have, which isn't working. Someone has to stand up and call for significant, decisive change.

Buy-in at the top

Having been working with these issues for over twenty-five years, I am not naïve enough to assume that department- or campus-wide programs to teach research processes will spring up everywhere simply because I wrote this book. What I have written is a clarion call to professors to take a serious look at the problem, engage resources to address it, and ultimately to win over departments and institutions.

This is a realm where the hard slog is more common than paths of ease.

Grassroots efforts do work if those at the grassroots have the will to move them up the ladder. Still, the opposition of an academic administration already hard-pressed to deliver good education can be a significant barrier. Administrators will not move from the status quo if there is any significant risk that a new approach will divert needed resources from the tasks that currently need to be accomplished.

Buy-in at the top is most likely to occur if the grassroots can show that disruption of current resources will be minimal and that costs can be kept within budgetary parameters. At the individual and departmental level, successful teaching of research processes can be accomplished with absolutely minimal financial commitment and little reconfiguration of personnel except for the academic librarians who will welcome the opportunity for a meatier role in academia.

Professors and departments need to demonstrate success first. To propose an untried idea is to risk almost certain murder of that idea by those in charge. To show a track record of success that has actually produced more engaged students and has cost few resources is to warm the heart of administrators who have trained themselves in the cold-heartedness needed to say "no" in order to keep the institution alive and thriving. The challenge is not, I believe, to divert huge resources to yet another bright idea but to show administrators that we can do a better job with, essentially, what we already have.

Why, then, call for administrative buy-in at all? For these reasons:

- *Administrators can set policy.* Here, we are not looking for mandates or decrees from above that will force professors to teach research processes. Rather, we require collaboratively generated statements of vision and practice that serve to redefine the department or administration along the lines of teaching research processes wherever possible. With such statements in place, departments and professors are much better protected from possible criticism and are given an incentive to develop research processes instruction. To say, "We teach research processes here," is to give everyone in the institution a rallying cry for implementation of plans actually to make that a reality.

- *Administrators can facilitate short- and long-term practice.* With upper level buy-in comes the opportunity to ask for the tools and support needed. This relates not just to starting up the initiatives that will make research processes instruction a reality but to sustaining such instruction in the long term. One of the greatest tragedies related to educational initiatives is that they tend to lose steam over time or vanish completely if their key champions leave the institution. An administration sold on a research processes' instruction vision can help ensure continued vitality of the work that is being done. A great idea without a plan to perpetuate it (and to modify it as times change) is doomed. Administrators can make sure the idea is sustainable.

- *Administrators can provide incentives.* A challenging fact in most of academia is that research is rewarded but teaching is less rewarded. There are few research grants to further learning and teaching, but many to support work done outside the classroom. Boyer (1990) has provided a pathway forward in this regard by arguing that scholarship is not merely discovery and integration. If members of the higher education community are advancing the cause of application and of teaching, these elements may also be called "scholarship." A true scholarship of teaching enables teaching professors to study and develop the teaching process itself.

How can an administrator provide resources for innovation in teaching such that faculty are given incentives for developing the teaching of research processes? It can first recognize such innovation as genuine scholarship. Second, it can provide research funding to professors who are willing to develop research processes' instructional philosophy and method. Third, it can recognize innovation in teaching as a strong factor in making tenure decisions. Fourth, it can encourage faculty (perhaps even financially) to attend conferences and write articles and books on teaching. Fifth, it can establish regularly issued awards to recognize significant innovations in teaching research processes.

What resources do we need?

We have the professors, the administrators, the academic librarians, the libraries, the databases, and all the other resources we require. Ultimately, the challenge is not to find resources but to marshal those resources and put them in a fresh direction. It comes down to priorities – what do we really want to accomplish?

Resourcing the enterprise is not nearly the daunting task that so many current educational initiatives seem to be. We do not need a Gates Foundation to give us ten million dollars, as much as we might appreciate the gift. While we may want to consider hiring a few more librarians and realigning research grants toward the scholarship of teaching, essentially we have most everything and everyone already at hand. Those resources just need to be prioritized in the direction of teaching research processes.

10

Conclusion

Abstract: The current deficiency in the teaching of research processes has far-reaching ramifications in the academy and the workplace. Can we call our graduates "educated" if they lack the ability to handle, with skill, the information of their disciplines? We have the resources to address the problem. What we need is the determination to do so.

Key words: information disasters; information handling.

It is tempting at this point to resort to clichéd language: "A thousand-mile journey begins with but a single step;" "A mighty fire begins with a single spark;" and so on. While these may express the message I wish to convey, they tend to trivialize the seriousness of the dilemma we are facing.

Many of our students don't know how to do research. They are going through undergraduate and even graduate studies as outsiders looking in, rarely really being able to participate in the discourse and discovery that their professors find so familiar. These same students do not even understand the expectations found in a standard research assignment (Head, 2008) and spend most of their "researching" time simply trying to follow professorial instructions while failing to grasp the methodology and never really engaging with the subject matter.

These students fail to appreciate the diversity of information sources available to them and lack the ability to evaluate these sources for quality and relevance. Overall, they handle whatever information they are dealing with clumsily and without significant understanding of the value of peer review and academic recognition in determining the weight to give to each work. They are truly outsiders, and they will remain so through much or all of their academic programs.

These students, at some point, will graduate and enter careers in industries, business or professions, where they will continue to show their limitations in working with the information that will be the life's blood of their occupations. In 2004, IDC, a major market intelligence organization, surveyed 600 industries in four sectors – financial services, government, manufacturing, and healthcare – to determine their costs for handling information. The resulting White Paper presented some startling statistics. For the average worker, the discovery and analysis of information, as of 2004, consumed 24 percent of working hours and cost each organization US$14,000 per worker per year. What is more, not finding needed information or having to retool or reformat existing information cost the average 1,000 employee organization over US$10,000,000 per year. The paper concludes:

> In this and other IDC studies, it has become obvious that tasks related to creating, organizing, finding, and analyzing information have become significant time sinks. The problem will only get worse as our economy migrates from being manufacturing-based to information-based. (Feldman and Duhi, 2005)

Today we have business graduates who lack the information skills that business practitioners themselves declare to be crucial (Klusek and Bornstein, 2006), consultants seeking information malpractice insurance to compensate for gaps in information handling ability (Ebbinghouse, 2000), and a steady stream of "information disasters" (Pidgeon and O'Leary, 2000), resulting in exploding space shuttles (Rogers, 1986), stock price crashes based on faulty research (Ojala, 2008), and needless deaths in the course of medical research (Rogers et al., 2001; Steinbrook, 2002).

Ultimately, we must pose the following, hopefully rhetorical, question: *Can we call our graduates "educated" if they lack the ability to handle with skill the information of their disciplines?* If our answer is "no," we will have to recognize that we have a significant problem on our hands. Even as information handling becomes a dominant element of daily life in the modern world, and the complexity of information is increasing exponentially, we have not yet recognized that our students lack research processes skills, let alone established workable means to address the problem.

The way forward need not tax our resources, as might, for example, our challenge with climate change. Higher education currently has the resources – personnel and finances – to teach research processes well and comprehensively. What we need is the will.

Paul Zurkowski (Zurkowsi and the National Commission on Libraries and Information Science, 1974) of the Information Industry Association estimated that only one-sixth of the American population was "information literate," that is, able to handle information to address issues and advance knowledge. His estimate is in all probability still valid today. If we live in an information age driven both by complex technology and a multitude of new types of information sources, this would appear to be simply not good enough.

Our universities are filled with confused, disengaged students looking into our disciplines from the outside and lacking an invitation to come in. We are graduating people who do not have the information-handling abilities needed to function well in their succeeding occupations. Society as a whole is questioning the value of the education we provide, and for good reason – we are using ages-old methods to tell our students *about* our disciplines without genuinely inviting them to learn the research processes that enable them actually to do *our* disciplines.

We do have a path forward. We now require the determination to travel that path.

References

ACRL (1989), *Presidential Committee on Information Literacy: Final Report.* Retrieved October 5, 2011 from *http://www.ala.org/ala/mgrps/divs/acrl/publications/whitepapers/presidential.cfm.*

ACRL (2000), *Information Literacy Competency Standards for Higher Education.* Retrieved October 2, 2011 from *http://www.ala.org/ala/mgrps/divs/acrl/standards/informationliteracycompetency.cfm.*

ACRL (2011), *Information Literacy in the Disciplines.* Retrieved October 2, 2011 from *http://wikis.ala.org/acrl/index.php/Information_literacy_in_the_disciplines.*

Andretta, S. (2007), "Information literacy: The functional literacy for the 21st century," in S. Andretta (ed.), *Change and Challenge: Information Literacy for the 21st Century* (pp. 1–14), Adelaide: Auslib Press.

Andretta, S., Pope, A., and Walton, G. (2008), "Information literacy education in the UK," *Communications in Information Literacy*, Vol. 2, No. 1, pp. 36–51. Retrieved October 3, 2011 from *http://www.comminfolit.org/index.php?journal=cil&page=article&op=view&path[]=Spring2008AR3&path[]=65.*

Anon (2004), "2003–2004 completed research grant projects (2004)," *Law Library Journal*, Vol. 6, No. 4, pp. 867–9.

A.N.T.S. (2011), *Animated Tutorial Sharing Project.* Retrieved October 2, 2011 from *http://ants.wetpaint.com/.*

Arum, R., and Roksa, J. (2011), *Academically Adrift: Limited Learning on College Campuses*, Chicago: University of Chicago Press.

Association of American Colleges and Universities (2009), *Information Literacy VALUE Rubric.* Retrieved October 2, 2011 from *http://www.aacu.org/value/rubrics/pdf/InformationLiteracy.pdf.*

Atherton, J. S. (2010), *Approaches to Study: "Deep" and "Surface."* Retrieved October 5, 2011 from *http://www.learningandteaching.info/learning/deepsurf.htm.*

Avdic, A., and Eklund, A. (2010), "Searching reference databases: What students experience and what teachers believe that students experience," *Journal of Librarianship and Information Science*, Vol. 42, No. 4, pp. 224–35. doi:10.1177/0961000610380119.

Badke, W. (2003), "All we need is a fast horse: Riding information literacy into the academy," in M.H. Raish (ed.), *Musings, Meanderings, and Monsters, Too: Essays on Academic Librarianship* (pp. 75–88), Lanham, MD: Scarecrow Press.

Badke, W. (2005), "Can't get no respect: Helping faculty to understand the educational power of information literacy," *Reference Librarian*, Vol. 43, No. 89, pp. 63–80. doi: 10.1300/J120v43n89_05.

Badke, W. (2009a), "Stepping beyond Wikipedia," *Educational Leadership*, Vol. 66, No. 6, pp. 54–8.

Badke, W. (2009b), "How we failed the Net generation," *Online*, Vol. 33, No. 4, pp. 47–9.

Badke, W. (2009c), "Ramping up the one-shot," *Online*, Vol. 33, No. 2, pp. 47–9. Retrieved October 5, 2011 from *http://www.allbusiness.com/education-training/literacy-illiteracy/11797610–1.html.*

Badke, W. (2010a), "Information as tool, not destination," *Online*, Vol. 34, No. 4, pp. 52–4.

Badke, W. (2010b), "Using a strategic approach to build coherence and relevance in credit information literacy courses," in C. Hollister (ed.), *Best Practices for Credit-Bearing Information Literacy Courses* (pp. 147–59), Chicago: Association of College and Research Libraries.

Badke, W. (2011a), *COMM 110 – Research Component*. Retrieved October 2, 2011 from *https://sites.google.com/site/williambadke2/COMM110Research*.

Badke, W. (2011b), *Research Strategies: Finding your Way through the Information Fog*, 4th edn, Bloomington, IN: iUniverse.com.

Badke, W. (2011c), "Why information literacy is invisible," *Communications in Information Literacy*, Vol. 4, No. 2, pp. 129–41. Retrieved from: *http://thebrowers.net/comminfolit/index.php?journal=cil&page=article&op=viewFile&path[]=Vol4-2010PER3&path[]=119*

Baker, R.K. (1997), "Faculty perceptions towards student library use in a large urban community college," *Journal of Academic Librarianship*, Vol. 23, No. 3, pp. 177–82.

Bennett, S. (2007), "Campus cultures fostering information literacy," *portal: Libraries and the Academy*, Vol. 7, No. 2, pp. 147–67.

Bent, M., and Stockdale, E. (2009), "Integrating information literacy as a habit of learning – assessing the impact of a thread of IL through the curriculum," *Journal of Information Literacy*, Vol. 3, No. 1, pp. 43–57. Retrieved October 2, 2011 from *http://ojs.lboro.ac.uk/ojs/index.php/JIL/article/view/PRA-V3-I1–2009-4/228*.

Berrett, D. (2011), "In for nasty weather," *Inside Higher Education*, May 16. Retrieved October 5, 2011 from *http://www.insidehighered.com/news/2011/05/16/life_for_college_professors_is_no_longer_what_it_once_was*.

Biggs, J. (1979), "Individual differences in study processes and the quality of learning outcomes," *Higher Education*, Vol. 8, No. 4, pp. 381–94.

Bodi, S. (2002), "How do we bridge the gap between what we teach and what they do? Some thoughts on the place of questions in the process of research," *Journal of Academic Librarianship*, Vol. 28, No. 3, pp. 109–14.

Boekhorst, A.K., and Horton, F.W. (2009), "Training-the-trainers in Information Literacy (TTT) Workshops Project, final report to UNESCO," *International Information and Library Review*, Vol. 41, No. 4, pp. 224–30.

Bouffard, M. (2001), "The scientific method, modernism, and postmodernism revisited: A reaction to Shephard (1999)," *Adapted Physical Activity Quarterly*, Vol. 18, No. 3, pp. 221–34.

Boyer, E.L. (1990), *Scholarship Reconsidered: Priorities of the Professoriate*, Princeton, NJ Carnegie Foundation for the Advancement of Teaching.

Brown, C. (2005), "Where do molecular biology graduate students find information?" *Science & Technology Libraries*, Vol. 25, No. 3, pp. 89–104. doi:10.1300/J122v25n03–06.

Brown, C.M. (1999), "Information literacy of physical science graduate students in the information age," *College and Research Libraries*, Vol. 60, No. 5, pp. 426–39. Retrieved September 27, 2011 from *http://crl.acrl.org/content/60/5/426.full.pdf+html*.

Brown, J.F., and Nelson, J.L. (2003), "Integration of information literacy into a revised medical school curriculum," *Medical Reference Services Quarterly*, Vol. 22, No. 3, pp. 63–74.

Brown, J.S., Collins, A., and Duguid, P. (1989), "Situated cognition and the culture of learning," *Educational Researcher*, Vol. 18, No. 1, pp. 32–42.

Bruce, C. (2001), "Faculty-librarian partnerships in Australian higher education: Critical dimensions," *Reference Services Review*, Vol. 29, No. 2, pp. 106–16.

Bundy, A. (2002), "Information literacy: The key competency for the 21st century," paper presented at the Annual Conference of the International Association of Technological University Libraries, Pretoria, South Africa (June). Retrieved September 27, 2011 from *http://eric.ed.gov/PDFS/ED434662.pdf.*

Bundy, A. (2004), *Australian and New Zealand Information Literacy Framework*, 2nd edn, Adelaide: Australian and New Zealand Institute for Information Literacy. Retrieved October 2, 2011 from *http://www.library.unisa.edu.au/learn/infolit/Infolit-2nd-edition.pdf.*

Bury, S. (2011), "Faculty attitudes, perceptions and experiences of information literacy: A study across multiple disciplines at York University, Canada," *Journal of Information Literacy*, Vol. 5, No. 1, pp. 45–64. Retrieved October 4, 2011 from *http://ojs.lboro.ac.uk/ojs/index.php/JIL/article/view/PRA-V5-I1–2011-1/1554.*

Caccavo, F. (2009), "Teaching undergraduates to think like scientists," *College Teaching*, Vol. 57, No. 1, pp. 9–14.

California State University (2007), *Information Competence Initiative*. Retrieved October 2, 2011 from *http://www.calstate.edu/LS/infocomp.shtml.*

Canadian Library Association (2005), *Rediscover the Library Moment: The Canadian Library Association's 60th Annual Conference and Trade Show, Calgary, Alberta, June 15–18, 2005*. Retrieved October 2, 2011 from *http://www.cla.ca/conference/2005/a_thursday.htm.*

Cannon, A. (1994), "Faculty survey on library research instruction," *RQ*, Vol. 33, No. 4, pp. 524–41.

Carpenter, B., and Tait, G. (2001), "The rhetoric and reality of good teaching: A case study across three faculties at the

Queensland University of Technology," *Higher Education*, Vol. 42, No. 2, pp. 191–203. Retrieved October 5, 2011 from *http://eprints.qut.edu.au/archive/00001391/02/1391. pdf.*

Carter, M. (2007), "Ways of knowing, doing, and writing in the disciplines," *CCC – National Council of Teachers of English*, Vol. 58, No. 3, pp. 385–418. Retrieved October 5, 2011 from *http://thelemming.com/lemming/POP-CULTURE/ways%20of%20knowing.pdf.*

Collier, P.J., and Morgan, D.L. (2008), "'Is that paper really due today?': Differences in first-generation and traditional college students' understandings of faculty expectations," *Higher Education*, Vol. 55, No. 4, pp. 425–46. Retrieved September 27, 2011 from *http://alabamafirst.ua.edu/ wp-content/uploads/2010/06/collier.pdf.*

Conclusions and Recommendations to UNESCO and CEI (draft) (2006), *Workshop on Information Literacy Initiative for Central and South East European Countries, Ljubjana, Slovenia, March 27–28, 2006.* Retrieved October 1, 2011 from *http://portal.unesco.org/ci/en/files/2 1870/11453537729Conclusions_and_recommendations_ Ljubjana_Meeting.doc/Conclusions%2Band%2Brecomm endations%2BLjubjana%2BMeeting.doc.*

Corrall, S. (2007), "Benchmarking strategic engagement with information literacy in higher education: Towards a working model," *Information Research*, Vol. 12, No. 4, pp. 12–14. Retrieved October 2, 2011 from *http://dialnet. unirioja.es/servlet/articulo?codigo=2390558&orden=138 911&info=link.*

Council of Europe, Council for Cultural Co-operation, Culture Committee (2000), *"New Information Technologies" Project: Training, Qualifications and New Professional Profiles: Draft Guidelines on Cultural Work within the Information Society*, Strasbourg: Council of

Europe. Retrieved September 27, 2011 from *http:// www.coe.int/t/dg4/cultureheritage/Resources/Texts/ CC-CULT(2000)49rev_EN.pdf?L=EN.*

Cronon, W. (1998), "Only connect. . .". *American Scholar,* Vol. 67, No. 4, p. 73.

Culp, K.M., Honey, M., and Mandinach, E. (2003), *A Retrospective on Twenty Years of Education Technology Policy,* U.S. Department of Education, Office of Educational Technology. Retrieved September 27, 2011 from *http://www.ed.gov/rschstat/eval/tech/20years.pdf.*

Dede, C. (2008), "A seismic shift in epistemology," *Educause Review,* Vol. 43, No. 3, pp. 80–1. Retrieved September 27, 2011 from *http://net.educause.edu/ir/library/pdf/ ERM0837.pdf.*

Ding, H. (2008), "The use of cognitive and social apprenticeship to teach a disciplinary genre: Initiation of graduate students into NIH grant writing," *Written Communication,* Vol. 25, No. 1, pp. 3–52.

Downes, S. (2006), *ACRLog: The Great (?) Debate: Is Information Literacy a Fad and a Waste of Time?,* July 4. Retrieved October 2, 2011 from *http://acrlog. org/2006/07/04/the-great-debate-is-information-literacy- a-fad-and-a-waste-of-time/.*

Dressen-Hammouda, D. (2008), "From novice to disciplinary expert: Disciplinary identity and genre mastery," *English for Specific Purposes,* Vol. 27, No. 2, pp. 233–52.

Duke, T.S., and Ward, J.D. (2009), "Preparing information literate teachers: A metasynthesis," *Library and Information Science Research,* Vol. 31, No. 4, pp. 247–56.

Ebbinghouse, C. (2000), "Disclaiming liability," *Searcher,* Vol. 8, No.3, pp. 61–6. Retrieved from *http://choo.fis. utoronto.ca/FIS/courses/LIS1325/Readings/ebbinghouse. pdf.*

Educational Testing Service (2006), *2006 ICT Literacy Assessment Preliminary Findings*, Princeton, NJ: Educational Testing Service. Retrieved September 27, 2011 from *http://www.ets.org/Media/Products/ICT_Literacy/pdf/2006_Preliminary_Findings.pdf*.

Ehrlinger, J., Johnson, K., Banner, M., Dunning, D., and Kruger, J. (2008), "Why the unskilled are unaware: Further explorations of (absent) self-insight among the incompetent," *Organizational Behavior and Human Decision Processes*, Vol. 105, No. 1, pp. 98–121.

Elmborg, J. (2006), "Critical information literacy: Implications for instructional practice," *The Journal of Academic Librarianship*, Vol. 32, No. 2, pp. 192–9.

Feder, T. (2005), "Cold fusion gets chilly encore," *Physics Today*, Vol. 58, No. 31. doi:10.1063/1.1881896. Retrieved October 5, 2011 from *http://scitation.aip.org/journals/doc/PHTOAD-ft/vol_58/iss_1/31_1.shtml*.

Feldman, D., and Sciammarella, S. (2000), "Both sides of the looking glass: Librarian and teaching faculty perceptions of librarianship at six community colleges," *College and Research Libraries*, Vol. 61, No. 6, pp. 491–8.

Feldman, S., and Duhi, J. (2005), "The hidden costs of information work," *IDC White Paper, March*. Retrieved October 6, 2011 from *http://www.scribd.com/doc/6138369/Whitepaper-IDC-Hidden-Costs-0405*.

First Year Information Literacy in the Liberal Arts Assessment (FYILLAA) (2008), Lawrence McKinley Gould Library, Carleton University. Retrieved September 27, 2011 from *http://apps.carleton.edu/campus/library/about/infolit/fyillaa/*.

Fischhoff, B., and MacGregor, D. (1986), "Calibrating databases," *Journal of the American Society for Information Science*, Vol. 37, No. 4, pp. 222–33.

Five Colleges of Ohio (2003), *Integrating Information Literacy into the Liberal Arts Curriculum*. Retrieved October 2, 2011 from *http://collaborations.denison.edu/ ohio5/grant/*.

Flanagin, A.J., Metzger, M.J., and Hartsell, E. (2010), *Kids and Credibility: An Empirical Examination of Youth, Digital Media Use, and Information Credibility*. Cambridge, MA: MIT Press. Retrieved September 27, 2011 from *http://mitpress.mit.edu/books/full_pdfs/Kids_ and_Credibility.pdf*.

Gallacher, I. (2007), "Who are those guys?: The results of a survey studying the information literacy of incoming law students," *California Western Law Review*, Vol. 44, pp. 1–47. Retrieved September 27, 2011 from *http://works.bepress.com/cgi/viewcontent. cgi?article=1000andcontext=ian_gallacher*.

Garner, S. (2006), *High-Level Colloquium on Information Literacy and Lifelong Learning, Bibliotheca Alexandrina, Alexandria, Egypt, November 6–9, 2005. Report of a Meeting Sponsored by the United Nations Education, Scientific, and Cultural Organisation (UNESCO), National Forum on Information Literacy (NFIL) and the International Federation of Library Associations and Institutions (IFLA)*. Retrieved October 2, 2011 from *http://www.ifla.org/III/wsis/High-Level-Colloquium.pdf*.

George, C., Bright, A., Hurlbert, T., Linke, E.C., Clair, G.S., and Stein, J. (2006), "Scholarly use of information: Graduate students' information seeking behaviour," *Information Research*, Vol. 11, No. 4, pp. 11–14. Retrieved October 7, 2011 from *http://informationr.net/ ir/11–4/paper272.html*.

Gilchrist, D.L. (2007), "Academic libraries at the center of instructional change: Faculty and librarian experience of library leadership in the transformation of teaching and learning," unpublished Ph.D., Oregon State University. Retrieved October 5, 2011 from *http:// ir.library.oregonstate.edu/jspui/bitstream/1957/5150/1/ gilchrist%20dissertation.pdf.*

Grant, D.M., Malloy, A.D., and Murphy, M.C. (2009), "A comparison of student perceptions of their computer skills to their actual abilities," *Journal of Information Technology Education*, Vol. 8, No. 141–60. Retrieved October 1, 2011 from *http://jite.org/documents/Vol8/ JITEv8p141–160Grant428.pdf.*

Greasley, P., and Cassidy, A. (2010), "When it comes round to marking assignments: How to impress and how to 'distress' lecturers . . .," *Assessment and Evaluation in Higher Education*, Vol. 35, No. 2, pp. 173–89.

Griffiths, J., and Brophy, P. (2005), "Student searching behavior and the Web: Use of academic resources and Google," *Library Trends*, Vol. 53, No. 4, pp. 539–54.

Gross, M., and Latham, D. (2009), "Undergraduate perceptions of information literacy: Defining, attaining, and self-assessing skills," *College and Research Libraries*, Vol. 70, No. 4, pp. 336–50.

Hall, L. (1999), "A home-grown program for raising faculty information competence," *Computers in Libraries*, Vol. 19, No. 8, pp. 28–30, 32, 34.

Hardesty, L. (1995), "Faculty culture and bibliographic instruction: An exploratory analysis," *Library Trends*, Vol. 44, No. 2, pp. 339–67.

Harris, T. (1993), "The post-capitalist executive: An interview with Peter F. Drucker," *Harvard Business Review*, Vol. 71, No. 3, pp. 114–22.

Hart Research Associates (2010), *Raising the Bar: Employers' Views on College Learning in the Wake of the Economic Downturn: A Survey among Employers Conducted on the Behalf of the Association of American*

Colleges and Universities. Washington, DC: Hart Research Associates. Retrieved October 5, 2011 from *http://www.aacu.org/leap/documents/2009_EmployerSurvey.pdf*.

Hase, S., and Kenyon, C. (2000), "From andragogy to heutagogy," *UltiBASE Articles*. Retrieved October 5, 2011 from *http://ultibase.rmit.edu.au/Articles/dec00/hase1.pdf*.

Hase, S., and Kenyon, C. (2007), "Heutagogy: A child of complexity theory," *Complicity: An International Journal of Complexity and Education*, Vol. 4, No. 1, pp. 111–18. Retrieved October 5, 2011 from *http://ejournals.library.ualberta.ca/index.php/complicity/article/view/8766/7086*.

Head, A.J. (2007), "Beyond Google: How do students conduct academic research?" *First Monday*, Vol. 12, No. 8. Retrieved October 4, 2011 from *http://www.uic.edu/htbin/cgiwrap/bin/ojs/index.php/fm/article/view/1998/1873*.

Head, A.J. (2008), "Information literacy from the trenches: How do humanities and social science majors conduct academic research?" *College and Research Libraries*, Vol. 69, No. 5, pp. 427–45. Retrieved September 27, 2011 from *http://crl.acrl.org/content/69/5/427.full.pdf+html*.

Head, A.J., and Eisenberg, M.B. (2009a), *Finding Context: What Today's College Students Say About Conducting Research in a Digital Age: Project Information Literacy Progress Report*. Retrieved September 27, 2011 from *http://www.libraryng.com/sites/libraryng.com/files/PIL_ProgressReport_2_2009.pdf*.

Head, A.J., and Eisenberg, M.B. (2009b), *Lessons Learned: How College Students Seek Information in the Digital Age: Project Information Literacy Progress Report*. Retrieved October 1, 2011 from *http://projectinfolit.org/pdfs/PIL_Fall2009_Year1Report_12_2009.pdf*.

Head, A.J., and Eisenberg, M.B. (2010), "Truth be told: How college students evaluate and use information in the digital age," *Seattle: University of Washington Information School, Project Information Literacy*. Retrieved October 4, 2011 from: *http://projectinfolit.org/pdfs/PIL_Fall2010_Survey_FullReport1.pdf*.

Head, A.J., and Eisenberg, M.B. (2011), "College students eager to learn but need help negotiating information overload," *The Seattle Times*, June 3. Retrieved October 5, 2011 from *http://seattletimes.nwsource.com/html/opinion/2015227485_guest05head.html; comments retrieved from http://community.seattletimes.nwsource. com/reader_feedback/public/display.php?source_name—base&source_id=2015227485*.

Healey, M., and Jenkins, A. (2009), *Developing Undergraduate Research and Inquiry*. York: The Higher Education Academy. Retrieved October 5, 2011 from *http://www.heacademy.ac.uk/assets/York/documents/resources/publications/DevelopingUndergraduate_Final.pdf*.

Heath, C., and Heath, D. (2010), *Switch: How to Change Things When Change Is Hard*. New York: Broadway Books.

Hicks, A., and Graber, A. (2010), "Shifting paradigms: Teaching, learning and web 2.0," *Reference Services Review*, Vol. 38, No. 4, pp. 621–33.

Hirsch, E.D. (2006), "Why do we have a knowledge deficit? (Policy perspectives, WestEd)," in *The Knowledge Deficit: Closing the Shocking Education Gap for American Children* (pp. 1–10) New York: Houghton Mifflin.

Hodge, D. (2007), "From convocation to capstone: Developing the student as scholar," Keynote address. Paper presented at the Association for American Colleges and Universities, The Student as Scholar: Undergraduate

Research and Creative Practice. Network for Academic Renewal Conference, April 2007, Long Beach, CA. Retrieved September 27, 2011 from *http://www.aacu.org/meetings/undergraduate_research/documents/Keynote.pdf*.

Horton Jr, F.W. (1983), "Information literacy vs. computer literacy," *Bulletin of the American Society for Information Science*, Vol. 9, No. 4, pp. 14–16.

Housewright, R., and Schonfeld, R. (2008), *Ithaka's 2006 Studies of Key Stakeholders in the Digital Transformation in Higher Education*. New York: Ithaka. Retrieved October 1, 2011 from *http://www.ithaka.org/research/Ithakas%20 2006%20Studies%20of%20Key%20Stakeholders%20 in%20the%20Digital%20Transformation%20in%20 Higher%20Education.pdf*.

Hrycaj, P., and Russo, R. (2007), "Reflections on surveys of faculty attitudes toward collaboration with librarians," *The Journal of Academic Librarianship*, Vol. 33, No. 6, pp. 692–6.

Hughes, H.E., Bruce, C.S., and Edwards, S.L. (2007), "Models for reflection and learning: A culturally inclusive response to the information literacy imbalance," in S. Andretta (ed.) *Change and Challenge: Information Literacy for the 21st Century* (pp. 59–84) Adelaide: Auslib Press.

Jenson, J.D. (2004), "It's the information age, so where's the information?" *College Teaching*, Vol. 52, No. 3, pp. 107–12.

Johnston, B., and Webber, S. (2003), "Information literacy in higher education: A review and case study," *Studies in Higher Education*, Vol. 28, No. 3, pp. 335–52.

Jones, E.A., Hoffman, S., and National Center for Education Statistics (1995), *National Assessment of College Student Learning: Identifying College Graduates' Essential Skills in Writing, Speech and Listening, and Critical Thinking:*

Final Project Report, Washington, DC: National Center for Education Statistics, U.S. Dept. of Education, Office of Educational Research and Improvement.

Kane, M., Berryman, S., Goslin, D., and Meltzer, A. (1990), *The Secretary's Commission on Achieving Necessary Skills: Identifying and Describing the Skills Required by Work*, Washington, DC: U.S. Department of Labor. Retrieved September 27, 2011 from *http://wdr.doleta.gov/ SCANS/idsrw/scansrep.pdf*.

Kapitzke, C. (2003), "Information literacy: a positivist epistemology and a politics of outformation," *Educational Theory*, Vol. 53, No. 1, pp. 37–53.

Katz, I.R. (2007), "ETS research finds college students fall short in demonstrating ICT literacy-national policy council to create national standards," *College and Research Libraries News*, Vol. 68, No. 1, p. 35. Retrieved September 27, 2011 from *http://crln.acrl.org/content/ 68/1/35.full.pdf*.

Katz, I.R., and Macklin, A.S. (2007), "Information and communication technology (ICT) literacy: Integration and assessment in higher education," *Systemics Cybernetics and Informatics*, Vol. 5, No. 4, pp. 50–5. Retrieved September 27, 2011 from *http://www.iiisci.org/ Journal/CV$/sci/pdfs/P890541.pdf*.

Kempcke, K. (2002), "The art of war for librarians: Academic culture, curriculum reform, and wisdom from Sun Tzu," *portal: Libraries and the Academy*, Vol. 2, No. 4, pp. 529–51.

Kennedy, G.E., Judd, T.S., Churchward, A., Gray, K., and Krause, K.L. (2008), "First year students' experiences with technology: Are they really digital natives?" *Australasian Journal of Educational Technology*, Vol. 24, No. 1, pp. 108–22. Retrieved September 27, 2011 from *http://www.ascilite.org.au/ajet/ajet24/kennedy.html*.

Kenny, S.S. (1998), *Reinventing Undergraduate Education: A Blueprint for America's Research Universities: The Boyer Commission on Educating Undergraduates in the Research University*. Retrieved October 5, 2011 from *http://naples.cc.sunysb.edu/pres/boyer.nsf/673918d46fbf 653e852565ec0056ff3e/d955b61ffddd590a852565ec005 717ae/$FILE/boyer.pdf*.

Keresztesi, M. (1982), "The science of bibliography: Theoretical implications for bibliographic instruction," in C. Oberman and K. Strauch (eds) *Theories of Bibliographic Education* (pp. 13–21), New York: Bowker.

Kirton, J., and Barham, L. (2005), "Information literacy in the workplace," *The Australian Library Journal*, Vol. 54, No. 4, pp. 365–76. Retrieved October 4, 2011 from: *http://www.alia.org.au/publishing/alj/54.4/alj.Vol_54_ No_04_2005.pdf#page=41*.

Klusek, L., and Bornstein, J. (2006), "Information literacy skills for business careers: Matching skills to the workplace," *Journal of Business and Finance Librarianship*, Vol. 11, No. 4, pp. 3–21.

Knight-Davis, S., and Sung, J.S. (2008), "Analysis of citations in undergraduate papers," *College and Research Libraries*, Vol. 69, No. 5, pp. 447–58.

Kruger, J., and Dunning, D. (1999), "Unskilled and unaware of it: How difficulties in recognizing one's own incompetence lead to inflated self-assessments," *Journal of Personality and Social Psychology*, Vol. 77, No. 6, pp. 1121–34.

Kuh, G.D., and Gonyea, R.M. (2003), "The role of the academic library in promoting student engagement in learning," *College and Research Libraries*, Vol. 64, No. 4, pp. 256–82.

Kuh, G.D., Kinzie, J., Buckley, J.A., Bridge, B.K., and Hayek, J.C. (2006), "What matters to student success: A review of the literature," commissioned report for the "National Symposium on Postsecondary Student Success: Spearheading a Dialog on Student Success," National Postsecondary Educational Cooperative. Retrieved September 27, 2011 from *http://nces.ed.gov/npec/pdf/kuh_team_report.pdf*.

Kuhlthau, C. (2011), *Information Search Process*. Retrieved October 4, 2011 from *http://www.scils.rutgers. edu/~kuhlthau/information_search_process.htm*.

Kuruppu, P.U., and Gruber, A.M. (2006), "Understanding the information needs of academic scholars in agricultural and biological sciences," *Journal of Academic Librarianship*, Vol. 32, No. 6, pp. 609–23.

Leckie, G.J. (1996), "Desperately seeking citations: Uncovering faculty assumptions about the undergraduate research," *Journal of Academic Librarianship*, Vol. 22, No. 3, pp. 201–8.

Leckie, G.J., and Fullerton, A. (1999a), "Information literacy in science and engineering undergraduate education: Faculty attitudes and pedagogical practices," *College & Research Libraries*, Vol. 60, No. 1, pp. 9–29.

Leckie, G.J., and Fullerton A. (1999b), "The roles of academic librarians in fostering a pedagogy for information literacy," 9th ACRL Conference, Detroit, Michigan, April 8–11, 1999. Retrieved October 1, 2011 from *http://0-www.ala.org.sapl.sat.lib.tx.us/ala/mgrps/divs/acrl/events/pdf/leckie99.pdf*.

LexisNexis 2010 International Workplace Productivity Survey (2010), Retrieved October 7, 2011 from *http://www.multivu.com/players/English/46619-LexisNexis-International-Workplace-Productivity-Survey/*.

Lilienfeld, S.O. (2011,), "Public skepticism of psychology: Why many people perceive the study of human behavior as unscientific," *American Psychologist*, June 13. Advance online publication. doi:10.1037/a0023963.

Lippincott, A., and Kuchida, H. (2005), *InfoIQ: A Service Offering of UCLA Anderson Computing and Information Services*. Retrieved September 27, 2011 from *http://repositories.cdlib.org/cgi/viewcontent.cgi?article=1048andcontext=anderson*.

Lippincott, J.K. (2005), "Net generation students and libraries," *Educause Review*, Vol. 40, No. 2, pp. 56–66. Retrieved September 27, 2011 from *http://net.educause.edu/ir/library/pdf/ERM0523.pdf*.

Liu, Z., and Yang, Z. (2004), "Factors influencing distance-education graduate students' use of information sources: A user study," *Journal of Academic Librarianship*, Vol. 30, No. 1, pp. 24–35.

Lloyd, A. (2010), "Framing information literacy as information practice: Site ontology and practice theory," *Journal of Documentation*, Vol. 66, No. 2, pp. 245–58. doi:10.1108/00220411011023643.

Lyotard, J-F. (1984), *The Postmodern Condition: A Report on Knowledge*. Minneapolis: University of Minnesota Press.

Maclellan, E. (2004), "How reflective is the academic essay?" *Studies in Higher Education*, Vol. 29, No. 1, pp. 75–89.

Marcum, J. (2002), "Rethinking information literacy," *Library Quarterly*, Vol. 72, No. 1, pp. 1–26.

Markless, S., and Streatfield, D. (2007), "Three decades of information literacy: Redefining the parameters," in S. Andretta (ed.), *Change and Challenge: Information Literacy for the 21st Century* (pp. 15–36), Adelaide: Auslib Press.

Martin, B. (1998), "The politics of research," in *Information Liberation: Challenging the Corruptions of Information Power* (pp. 123–42), London: Freedom Press. Retrieved October 4, 2011 from *http://www.uow.edu.au/~bmartin/pubs/98il/il07.pdf*.

Marton, F., and Säljö, R. (1976a), "On qualitative differences in learning. I. Outcome and process," *British Journal of Educational Psychology*, Vol. 46, No. 1, pp. 4–11.

Marton, F., and Säljö, R. (1976b), "On qualitative differences in learning. II. Outcome as a function of the learner's conception of the task," *British Journal of Educational Psychology*, Vol. 46, No. 2, pp. 115–27.

Massey-Burzio, V. (1998), "From the other side of the reference desk: A focus group study," *Journal of Academic Librarianship*, Vol. 24, No. 3, pp. 208–15.

Maughan, P.D. (2001), "Assessing information literacy among undergraduates: A discussion of the literature and the University of California-Berkeley assessment experience," *College and Research Libraries*, Vol. 62, No. 1, pp. 71–85.

McEuen, S.F. (2001), "How fluent with information technology (FIT) are our students?" *Educause Quarterly*, Vol. 24, No. 4, pp. 8–17. Retrieved September 27, 2011 from *http://net.educause.edu/ir/library/pdf/eqm0140.pdf*.

McGuinness, C. (2006), "What faculty think: Exploring the barriers to information literacy development in undergraduate education," *The Journal of Academic Librarianship*, Vol. 32, No. 6, pp. 573–82.

McGuire, W.J. (1972), "Attitude change: The information-processing paradigm," in C. McClintock (ed.), *Experimental Social Psychology* (pp. 108–41) New York: Holt, Rinehart and Winston.

McNeil, B.J., Elfrink, V., Beyea, S.C., Pierce, S.T., and Bickford, C.J. (2006), "Computer literacy study: Report of qualitative findings," *Journal of Professional Nursing: Official Journal of the American Association of Colleges of Nursing*, Vol. 22, No. 1, pp. 52–9.

Melville, D. (2009), *Higher Education in a Web 2.0 World: Report of an Independent Committee of Inquiry into the*

Impact on Higher Education of Students' Widespread Use of Web 2.0 Technologies, Bristol: Committee of Inquiry into the Changing Learner Experience.

Middle States Commission on Higher Education (2003), *Developing Research and Communication Skills: Guidelines for Information Literacy in the Curriculum*. Philadelphia: Middle States Commission on Higher Education. Retrieved October 2, 2011 from *http://www.msche.org/publications/Developing-Skills080111151714.pdf*.

Middle States Commission on Higher Education (2009), *Characteristics of Excellence in Higher Education: Eligibility Requirements and Standards for Accreditation*. Retrieved October 1, 2011 from *http://www.msche.org/publications/CHX06_Aug08REVMarch09.pdf*.

Mittermeyer, D., and Quirion, D. (2003), *Information Literacy: Study of Incoming First-Year Undergraduates in Quebec*. Retrieved September 27, 2011 from *http://www.crepuq.qc.ca/documents/bibl/formation/studies_Ang.pdf*.

Mutch, A. (1999), "Critical realism, managers and information," *British Journal of Management*, Vol. 10, No. 4, pp. 323–33.

Nichols, J.T. (2009), "The 3 directions: Situated information literacy," *College and Research Libraries*, Vol. 70, No. 6, pp. 515–30.

O'Connor, L., and Newby, J. (2011), "Entering unfamiliar territory: Building an information literacy course for graduate students in interdisciplinary areas," *Reference and User Services Quarterly*, Vol. 50, No. 3, pp. 224–9.

Oakleaf, M. (2009), "Using rubrics to assess information literacy: An examination of methodology and interrater reliability," *Journal of the American Society for Information Science and Technology*, Vol. 60, No. 5, pp. 969–83.

Oakleaf, M., and Kaske, N. (2009), "Guiding questions for assessing information literacy in higher education," *portal: Libraries and the Academy*, Vol. 9, No. 2, pp. 273–86.

Obama, B. (2009), *National Information Literacy Awareness Month, 2009, by the President of the United States of America: A Proclamation*. Retrieved October 2, 2011 from *http://www.whitehouse.gov/the_press_office/ Presidential-Proclamation-National-Information-Literacy-Awareness-Month/*.

Oblinger, D.G., and Hawkins, B.L. (2006), "The myth about student competency," *Educause Review*, Vol. 41, No. 2. Retrieved October 1, 2011 from *http://www.educause. edu/ir/library/pdf/ERM0627.pdf*.

Ojala, M. (2008), "The unfriendly skies of computer glitches and human error," *Online*, Vol. 32, No. 6, p. 5.

Ontario (Canada) Confederation of University Faculty Associations (2009), "Students less prepared for university education," *Ontario University Report*, Vol. 3, No. 1. Retrieved October 3, 2011 from *http://notes.ocufa.on.ca/ OntarioUniversityReport.nsf/0/EE9751D6CD86DEB4 85257590005738F4?OpenDocument*.

Pan, B., Hembrooke, H., Joachims, T., Lorigo, L., Gay, G., and Granka, L. (2007), "In Google we trust: Users' decisions on rank, position, and relevance," *Journal of Computer-Mediated Communication*, Vol. 12, No. 3, pp. 801–23.

Partnership for 21st Century Skills (2009), *The MILE Guide: Milestones for Improving Learning and Education*. Tucson, AZ: Partnership for 21st Century Skills. Retrieved September 27, 2011 from *http://www.21stcenturyskills. org/documents/MILE_Guide_091101.pdf*.

Pedler, M., Burgoyne, J., and Boydell, T. (1991), *The Learning Company: A Strategy For Sustainable Development*. London: McGraw-Hill.

Perrett, V. (2004), "Graduate information literacy skills: The 2003 ANU skills audit," *Australian Library Journal*, Vol. 53, No. 2, pp. 161–72. Retrieved September 27, 2011 from *http://alia.org.au/publishing/alj/53.2/full.text/perrett.html*.

Peters, M. (1995), "Education and the postmodern condition: Re-visiting Jean-François Lyotard," *Journal of Philosophy of Education*, Vol. 29, No. 3, pp. 387–400.

Pidgeon, N., and O'Leary, M. (2000), "Man-made disasters: Why technology and organizations (sometimes) fail," *Safety Science*, Vol. 34, No. 1–3, pp. 15–30.

Primary Research Group (2008), *College Information Literacy Efforts Benchmarks*. New York: Primary Research Group.

Programme for International Student Assessment (2005), *The Definition and Selection of Key Competencies: Executive Summary*. Geneva: OECD. Retrieved September 27, 2011 from *http://www.oecd.org/dataoecd/47/61/35070367.pdf*.

Randall, R.,. Smith, J., Clark, K., and Foster, N. (2008), *The Next Generation of Academics: A Report of a Study Conducted at the University of Rochester*. Rochester, NY: University of Rochester Libraries. Retrieved September 27, 2011 from *http://hdl.handle.net/1802/6053*.

Ren, W. (2000), "Library instruction and college student self-efficacy in electronic information searching," *Journal of Academic Librarianship*, Vol. 26, No. 5, pp. 323–8.

Response to Barbara Fister [Anonymous] (2011), "Why the research paper isn't working." Retrieved September 27, 2011 from *http://www.insidehighered.com/blogs/library_babel_fish/why_the_research_paper_isn_t_working#Comments*.

Riordan, T. (2008), "Disciplinary expertise revisited: The scholarship of teaching and learning philosophy," *Arts and Humanities in Higher Education: An International*

Journal of Theory, Research and Practice, Vol. 7, No. 3, pp. 262–75.

Rogers, M., Oder, N., and Albanese, A. (2001), "Could librarians' help have prevented Hopkins tragedy?" *Library Journal*, Vol. 126, No. 14, p. 16.

Rogers, W. (1986), *Report of the Presidential Commission on the Space Shuttle Challenger Accident*. National Aeronautics and Space Administration. Retrieved from *http://history.nasa.gov/rogersrep/genindex.htm*.

Rosenblatt, S. (2010), "They can find it but they don't know what to do with it: Describing the use of scholarly literature by undergraduate students," *Journal of Information Literacy*, Vol. 4, No. 2, pp. 50–61. Retrieved September 27, 2011 from *http://ojs.lboro.ac.uk/ojs/index.php/JIL/article/view/LLC-V4-I2-2010-1/1506*.

Saunders, L. (2009), "The future of information literacy in academic libraries: A Delphi study," *portal: Libraries and the Academy*, Vol. 9, No. 1, pp. 99–114.

SCONUL Working Group on Information Literacy (2011), *The SCONUL Seven Pillars Of Information Literacy: Core Model for Higher Education*. London: Society of College, National and University Libraries. Retrieved October 2, 2011 from *http://www.sconul.ac.uk/groups/information_literacy/publications/coremodel.pdf*.

Selwyn, N. (2007), "The use of computer technology in university teaching and learning: A critical perspective," *Journal of Computer Assisted Learning*, Vol. 23, pp. 83–94.

Shen, Y. (2007), "Information seeking in academic research: A study of the sociology faculty at the University of Wisconsin-Madison," *Information Technology & Libraries*, Vol. 26, No. 1, pp. 4–13.

Shephard, R.J. (2001), "The scientific method, modernism, and postmodernism revisited: A response to Bouffard

(2001)," *Adapted Physical Activity Quarterly*, Vol. 18, No. 3, pp. 235–9.

Singleton-Jackson, J., Lumsden, D.B., and Newsom, R. (2009), "Johnny still can't write, even if he goes to college: A study of writing proficiency in higher education graduate students," *Current Issues in Education*, Vol. 12, No. 10. Retrieved September 27, 2011 from *http://cie.asu.edu/ojs/index.php/cieatasu/article/viewFile/45/9*.

Steinbrook, R. (2002), "Protecting research subjects: The crisis at Johns Hopkins," *New England Journal of Medicine*, Vol. 346, No. 9, pp. 716–20.

Sterngold, A.H. (2008), "Rhetoric versus reality: A faculty perspective on information literacy instruction," in J.M. Hurlbert (ed.), *Defining Relevancy: Managing the New Academic Library* (pp. 85–95), Westport, CT: Libraries Unlimited.

Stoan, S.K. (1984), "Research and library skills: An analysis and interpretation," *College and Research Libraries*, Vol. 45, No. 2, pp. 99–109.

Stoan, S.K. (1991), "Research and information retrieval among academic researchers: Implications for library instruction," *Library Trends*, Vol. 39, No. 3, pp. 238–58. Retrieved October 1, 2011 from *http://www.ideals.illinois.edu/bitstream/handle/2142/7725/librarytrendsv39i3g_opt.pdf?sequence=1*.

Stone, J.A., and Madigan, E. (2007), "Inconsistencies and disconnects," *Communications of the ACM*, Vol. 50, No. 4, pp. 76–9.

Sturges, P., and Gastinger, A. (2010), "Information literacy as a human right," *Libri: International Journal of Libraries & Information Services*, Vol. 60, No. 3, pp. 195–202. doi:10.1515/libr.2010.017.

Svensson, L. (1977), "On qualitative differences in learning. III. Study skill and learning," *British Journal* of *Educational Psychology*, Vol. 47, No. 3, pp. 233–43.

The Big Blue: *Information Skills for Students*. Retrieved November 15, 2011 from *http://www.leeds.ac.uk/bigblue/onlineiscourses.html*.

The Prague Declaration: *"Towards an Information Literate Society." Information Literacy Meeting of Experts, Prague, 20–23 September, 2003*. Retrieved October 2, 2011 from *http://portal.unesco.org/ci/en/files/19636/1122 8863531PragueDeclaration.pdf/PragueDeclaration.pdf*.

University College London (UCL) CIBER Group (2008), *Information Behaviour of the Researcher of the Future*, CIBER Briefing Paper No. 9, London: University College London. Retrieved September 27, 2011 from *http://www.jisc.ac.uk/media/documents/programmes/reppres/gg_final_keynote_11012008.pdf*.

University of Alberta. Augustana Campus (2007), *It Changed the Way I Do Research: Period [video]*. Retrieved October 2, 2011 from *http://www.library.ualberta.ca/augustana/infolit/video/*.

University of Alberta. Augustana Campus (2011), *Augustana Information Literacy*. Retrieved October 2, 2011 from *http://www.library.ualberta.ca/augustana/infolit/*.

Valentine, B. (2001), "The legitimate effort in research papers: Student commitment versus faculty expectations," *Journal of Academic Librarianship*, Vol. 27, No. 2, pp. 107–15.

Wang, Y., and Artero, M. (2005), "Caught in the Web: University student use of Web resources," *Educational Media International*, Vol. 42, No. 1, pp. 71–82.

Webber, S., and Johnston, B. (2000), "Conceptions of information literacy: New perspectives and implications," *Journal of Information Science*, Vol. 26, No. 6, pp. 381–97.

Webber, S. and Johnston, B. (2006), "Working towards the information literate university," in G. Walton and A. Pope (eds), *Information Literacy: Recognising the Need. Staffordshire University, Stoke-on-Trent: 17 May 2006* (pp. 47–58), Oxford: Chandos. Retrieved October 1, 2011 from *http://dis.shef.ac.uk/sheila/staffs-webber-johnston.pdf.*

Weetman, J. (2005a), "Osmosis — Does it work for the development of information literacy?" *Journal of Academic Librarianship*, Vol. 31, No. 5, pp. 456–60.

Weetman, J. (2005b), "The 'Seven pillars of wisdom' model: A case study to test academic staff perceptions," *SCONUL Focus*, Vol. 34, pp. 31–6.

Williams, D., and Wavell, C. (2007), "Secondary school teachers' conceptions of student information literacy," *Journal of Librarianship and Information Science*, Vol. 39, No. 4, pp. 199–212.

Yi, S. (2007), "Information seeking in academic research: A study of the sociology faculty at the University of Wisconsin-Madison," *Information Technology and Libraries*, Vol. 26, No. 1, pp. 4–13.

Zurkowski, P., and National Commission on Libraries and Information Science (1974), *The Information Service Environment Relationships and Priorities. Related Paper No. 5.* (ERIC Document Reproduction Service No. ED100391.) Retrieved October 2, 2011 from *http://www.eric.ed.gov/PDFS/ED100391.pdf.*

Index

Accreditors 67–68

ACRL Information Literacy
Standards 75–78

Administrators, Academic 84–86,
175–177, 186–190

Australian and New Zealand
Information Literacy
Framework 76–77

Constructivism 116–122

Critical thinking 20, 27, 34, 66,
111–113, 118, 124–125,
127, 187

Departments, Academic 170–175

Disciplines, Academic
In general 8–9, 13–16, 82,
93–114, 122–137,
164–165
Humanities 141–147
Professional programs
158–161
Sciences 153–157
Social Sciences 147–153

Epistemology 11–16, 94–97

Faculty
Assumptions about Research
Processes Education 50–54

Culture 62–66
Educational task 162–170
Expectations 2–7
Perception of Librarians 67
Skills in Research Processes/
Information Literacy
44–46

Heath and Heath, *Switch*
171–177

Higher education
Mission 21–22

Information
"Cheap commodity" xlv, 117,
119, 124, 174–175
Classification 13–16
Definition 10

Information based instruction
165–166

Information literacy
Blind spot in higher education
xiii, 91
Credit-based courses 81–83
Definition 1–24, 74–78
Educational requirement xiv,
191–194
Goals 22–24, 116
Remedial instruction 50–54,
78–81, 184

Skills required 9–20
Standards 17, 74–78
Student inability 32–43
Through the curriculum
    approaches 84–86
Workplace 192–193

Librarians
And credit-bearing research
    courses 82–83
And student assignments
    111–113
And faculty culture 62–66
As process experts 135,
    140–141
Collaboration with faculty
    125–126, 145, 168, 174
Development of information
    literacy standards 74–78
Experience with student
    difficulties xv, 26–27, 174
Faculty perception of 67
Realigning the work of
    183–185
Remedial research processes
    instruction 50–51
Teaching database searching
    135, 147, 152, 157, 161

Metanarrative 104–107, 143–144,
    149–150, 155–156,
    159–160
Modular assignments 145–147,
    151–153, 157, 166–168

Research
Definitions 7–9
Research model 97–102
Skills required 9–20
Research Processes
Autobiography 128, 164–165,
    186–187
Case studies 139–162
Classroom 115–137
Content instruction 136–137
Definition 24, 116
Disciplinary thinking 91–114,
    129–131
Research model 97–102
Skill development,
    Disciplinary
    131–136
Student inability 32–43
Resources (Finances and
    Personnel) 179–190

SCONUL Seven Pillars of
    Information Literacy
    model 17, 77–78
Students
Pre-University 27–32
Graduate students 36–43
University 32–36

Technology 18–20, 60–62

Writing, Academic 2–7

Zurkowski, Paul 71–74, 193

371.3
B136

127857

CPSIA information can be obtained at www.ICGtesting.com
Printed in the USA
BVOW02s0832221013

334351BV00007B/298/P

3 4711 00218 5074